THE
QUICK AFTER-WORK
FRENCH
❖ *Cookbook* ❖

THE
QUICK AFTER-WORK
FRENCH
❖ *Cookbook* ❖

HILAIRE WALDEN

PIATKUS

First published in 1994 by
Judy Piatkus (Publishers) Ltd
5 Windmill St, London W1P 1HF

The moral right of the author has been asserted
A catalogue record for this book is available from the British Library

ISBN 0-7499-1426-2

Designed by Paul Saunders
Photographs by Martin Brigdale
Food for photography prepared by Meg Janz
Photographic styling by Roisin Nield
Illustrations by David Downton

Set in Stempel Garamond by
Phoenix Photosetting, Chatham, Kent
Printed and bound in Great Britain by
Butler & Tanner Ltd, Frome, Somerset

CONTENTS

Introduction

When most of us think of French cooking we think of *haute cuisine* or large pots of slow-simmered, deeply flavoured stews, but these are both styles that have little relevance for most contemporary French people. Like us, the French are turning to quickly cooked dishes, at least during the week. This does not rule out some of their long-standing favourites, such as Leeks Vinaigrette and Celeriac Rémoulade. Nor does it mean they have lost their love of cooking or eating good food.

French cooks have always had a seemingly inborn ability to make the most of ingredients. They know how to cook them sympathetically, and how to use herbs to enhance flavours. They also naturally expect quality in their ingredients, which means freshness and flavour and not just uniform appearance and size. Because quality is expected, quality is provided.

French food is accessible and familiar to the majority of people in Britain. Therefore, these dishes will be readily accepted by all but the most conservative of eaters, and no exotic or unusual ingredients will have to be searched for.

For me, 'quick cooking' is not just about recipes that can be prepared quickly, they must also cook quickly. And sometimes I just want something that does not require me to do very much. After a quick bit of assembly I want the dish to cook on its own ('hands off' rather than 'hands on'), leaving me free to put my feet up, have a bath or a drink, or talk to friends. On these occasions I often choose recipes that are cooked in the oven. Although they may take a little longer, once in the oven they can be left to cook unattended. Similarly, soups are trouble-free, as they can be left to bubble gently on the stove.

All the same, I still expect dishes to taste good. I take short cuts or cut corners but I never sacrifice quality; no artificial contrivances for the sake of saving 5 minutes. I prefer to use recipes that genuinely cook in less time rather than modifying longer-cooking dishes so much that they lose their character.

TIPS FOR COOKING QUICKLY

A few simple actions can hasten and ease the whole process of preparing a meal, and in a short time they will become second nature.

First check that you have all the necessary ingredients, and remove meat, fish, eggs, milk, etc, from the refrigerator. Read through the recipe so you have a good idea of what you have to do. This will help you avoid wasting time later by constantly having to refer back to the recipe. You will also know which ingredients to prepare first, which can be prepared while the others cook, and whether it is necessary to heat any water, for example, for cooking vegetables.

Small pieces of food obviously cook more quickly than large ones, and diced butter melts more quickly, and evenly, than a lump. Young vegetables cook faster than older ones.

Temperature is another obvious, yet sometimes unconsidered, factor. I always use meat, poultry, fish, eggs and butter that are at room temperature; if you take one of these items from the refrigerator and cook it right away, you will have to allow extra time for it to cook.

I find steaming a useful cooking method because food doesn't overcook as quickly, and can be left quite happily in the steaming basket for a short while until required. Foods cooked *en papillote* (in parcels) have the added attraction of no cooking pot or serving dish to wash up. Steamed vegetables have the further advantages of being drier than boiled ones (this is particularly true of leeks, asparagus and broccoli) and can be served straight from the steaming basket without the need for straining.

Metal steaming baskets are inexpensive. Or you can improvise with a colander, providing the volume of food is small enough for it not to be crowded and piled high.

If cooking more than one dish, choose recipes whose preparation and cooking fit together rather than clash. For instance, if a first course needs to be prepared and cooked immediately before it is eaten, choose a main course that can be left to cook unattended. If a main course needs last-minute attention, accompany it with a vegetable that requires none, or a salad.

Finally, to save time and washing up, try to serve food in the pan or dish in which it was cooked.

The measurements in the following recipes were correct to my taste, and that of my friends, when I tested them. But the flavour of fresh ingredients is not constant, branded goods vary in taste, and everyone has their own particular preferences. So please always taste dishes as you are making them, and before serving them. Having used my recipes, I hope you will feel inspired to make your own adaptations and add your own ideas.

Cooking times can also vary according to the particular ingredients, their temperature at the start of cooking, and the cooking equipment. I use an oven thermometer but, as oven temperatures can be notoriously fickle, you may find that you have to adjust cooking times according to the whims of your oven. Even so, all the dishes in this book should be ready to eat in less than about 30 minutes.

INGREDIENTS

One of the attractions of French cooking is that all the ingredients can be found in a good supermarket with a wet fish counter, although I would recommend finding a good butcher and fishmonger rather than buying 'average' supermarket meat and fish. In fact, quite a number of my preferred products are French, such as butter and vinegar, because of their superior quality. France also produces the best mustards, unless you want a more fiery, less flavourful product, in which case England takes the honours with her traditional mustard.

Basic items
You do not need a very large stock of basic ingredients for the recipes in the *Quick After-Work French Cookbook*, and you may well have them all already. My main basic items are:

Butter French unsalted creamery butter, not just because of the better initial quality, but because it will be fresh. (Salted butter is usually more ancient because the salt is used to preserve as well as flavour it.) Unsalted butter is also better for cooking as it contains less sediment and is therefore less likely to burn.

Oils I usually use a mild (which is not synonymous with inferior bland) French olive oil for cooking, and a fruity virgin oil for salads and tossing with vegetables. I also sometimes have a flavourless groundnut oil which I use for frying when I do not want to detect the flavour of the oil. I also have a small can or bottle of walnut oil and perhaps a hazelnut oil, to go with salads and cheeses.

Home-made herb oils add instant character, whether used for cooking, salad dressings or tossing vegetables. To make them, half fill a bottle or jar with fresh herbs such as basil, tarragon, thyme or rosemary, and fill the bottle or jar completely with a mild oil. Put on the lid and leave for 2–4 weeks, shaking occasionally. Alternatively, flavour the oil with a few rosemary sprigs or chillies, or several garlic cloves.

Vinegars Good-quality white and red French wine vinegars are reliably better than their English equivalents. (For really special occasions I splash out on those from Martin Pouret, the only company still making wine vinegars by the old method of ageing in oak barrels; they are available from good delicatessens and supermarkets and Crabtree and Evelyn.) Sherry vinegar also has a place, as it adds depth to salad dressings.

Mustard Jars of Dijon, stronger Bordeaux, French tarragon and wholegrain Meaux mustard (French wholegrain mustards are generally milder than English ones) can invariably be found on my cupboard shelves.

Wine It is not worth cooking with a wine that you would not be happy to drink, or the dregs left in the bottom of opened bottles. A cheap, thin, acidic wine will be as unpleasant in a cooked dish as it is to drink.

The effect a wine has on a dish is related to its body, so I usually use medium-bodied (by which I do not mean medium sweet or medium dry) wines.

Wine left in a bottle keeps better if allowed minimum contact with air, and kept cool, so pour it into bottles of an appropriate size, close them tightly and keep in the refrigerator. Or invest in a special device that pumps the air out of the partly used bottle to keep the wine fresh.

Canned Goods The canning process takes its toll on the quality of many foods. Some exceptions are flageolet beans, haricot beans and chick peas. I am not very keen on the taste of canned tomatoes, so I prefer to boost the flavour of fresh ones if necessary with passata. (Passata, made from sieved plum tomatoes, is packed in bottles and cartons. It therefore tastes much fresher than canned tomatoes and does not have a 'tinny' taste.)

Pastes/Jars Pesto, sun-dried tomatoes, sun-dried tomato purée and passata.

Fresh Ingredients

Tomatoes After suffering a number of years of flavourless hot-house ones, we are now being offered an increasing choice of tomatoes that have been especially selected for their flavour. When these are also allowed to ripen in the sun, we start getting back to what tomatoes should taste like.

Garlic Garlic is almost synonymous with French cooking, but the amount you use is up to you, bearing in mind that, because the cooking is quick, the flavour of the garlic will be almost at its height. (The longer and gentler the cooking, the more the flavour mellows.) I buy loose bulbs rather than those packed in cardboard boxes, as I have found they keep better. Choose bulbs that have plump, firm cloves, keep them in a cool, dry, airy place, and remove any traces of green shoots as they taste bitter.

Herbs With the exception of oregano, which is actually better when dried in bunches, I use fresh herbs. Supermarkets now sell them growing in pots, as well as cut in packets. It is also very easy to grow your own basic herbs, such as parsley and chives, even if you do not have a garden. Pots on the windowsill will suffice.

However, if fresh herbs are not available, use freeze-dried or frozen rather than dried. With the exception of oregano, herbs do not dry well.

The flavour of fresh herbs varies in strength, so it is important to taste each herb before it is used to judge its potency. Then taste the dish before serving to make sure you have added enough.

I use flat-leaved continental parsley.

Stock If you do not feel inclined to make full-scale stocks, it's very easy to make simple versions. For example, whenever I have chicken skin and bones I simmer them immediately in water with an onion, carrot, perhaps a stick of celery, and a bouquet garni, for 20–40 minutes. Then, if I don't need the stock in the next day or so, I freeze it. Alternatively, if I don't want to make this 'quick' stock, I freeze the skin and bones for use later.

Vegetable stock is easily made by softening and lightly browning an onion in oil, then adding chopped leek, carrot and celery, some mushroom stalks and peelings, some tomato skins and seeds, and a bunch of herbs. Cover with water and simmer for 20–40 minutes.

If I do not have any home-made stock, I buy chilled stock from the supermarket; I do not use stock cubes.

Crème Fraîche   Crème fraîche is the standard cream used in France and contributes an essential flavour. It has a fresher, slightly sharper taste than double cream, but is less sharp than soured cream. It has a minimum fat content of 35 per cent and does not separate when boiled. It is now sold in many supermarkets and specialist food shops, but you can make your own by gently heating 2 parts double cream to 1 part buttermilk, soured cream or plain yogurt to 30°C/85°F. Then pour into a container, partially cover, and leave at room temperature for 6–8 hours or until thickened. Some of this crème fraîche can be used in place of the buttermilk to make a new batch of crème fraîche, if liked.

The quick alternative to crème fraîche is to combine Greek yogurt with 8 per cent fat fromage frais. (By the way, the measurement of fat in dairy products is not the same in France and Britain: 8 per cent fat in a French product would be 8 per cent of the whole product, whereas in Britain it would be 8 per cent of the dry matter, therefore excluding water.)

I have suggested an alternative to crème fraîche where I think one can be used; the alternatives vary, depending on the recipe.

Soft Cheese   This refers to unripened cheese with a soft, spreadable texture, and no rind. There are many types, with variable fat contents, and unless I specify a type in a recipe, you can use a soft cheese of your choice – for example ricotta, cream cheese or curd cheese.

Lardons   Lardons are cubes of pork, usually cut from a smoked breast. French lardons are now available in vacuum packs in a few specialist shops in Britain. There are also packs of English lardons, which are unsmoked, mild and on the moist side. As an alternative to buying lardons, ask a butcher or delicatessen assistant to cut 2.5cm (1inch) thick slices of good-quality streaky bacon. Cut them into strips vertically when you get home.

Eggs The diet of the hens and the freshness of the eggs really do affect the taste of the eggs, particularly in simple dishes such as Baked Eggs en Cocotte. I therefore frequently buy eggs from a free-range flock that I know. This also gives me the confidence to use the eggs raw, as in Chocolate Mousse, or to cook them lightly, as in Spinach and Poached Egg Salad or Poached Eggs on Grilled Field Mushrooms.

Bread It's now easy to buy long loaves labelled 'French bread', but it is more difficult to buy bread that really resembles the genuine article. Needless to say, it is well worth searching for.

For savoury toast, dunking into soups and mopping up cooking juices, I use firm-textured country bread.

For sweet toast, I use buttery brioche (which can be kept fresh in a polythene bag in the fridge).

EQUIPMENT

As with ingredients, you will only need a few familiar items of equipment. And what you need should be related to the amount and complexity of your cooking. For example, sometimes a mandoline can be more practical than a food processor (see below).

This is not a definitive list; it just covers items that I think merit a few words:

Knives Professional cooks always stress the importance of good knives, but if you are cooking for one or two people and the amount of cooking you do is quite limited, it is possible to get by with one all-purpose knife with a fairly slim blade about 15cm (6 inches) long, providing it is sharp. This is especially true if you have a food processor or mandoline for vegetable slicing, etc. However it does make life easier, and food preparation quicker, if you have at least a couple of good-quality sharp knives.

Strong Kitchen Scissors I have always found kitchen scissors useful, but until I damaged my left hand and was unable to use it for quite a while, I did not realise just how versatile they are, if a little slow. They come in handy for all sorts of tasks, ranging from snipping herbs to cutting vegetables into smaller pieces as they cook in a saucepan, to speed their cooking.

Double-handed Herb Chopper (also known by the Italian name of *mezzaluna*) This has a wide, curved stainless steel blade with a handle at each end. The chopper is useful for cutting herbs, garlic, onions, etc, especially if you are not very adept with a knife.

Mandoline Slicer/Grater   This has adjustable steel blades – one rippled, one straight – mounted on a wooden, metal or plastic base, and can be used for slicing and grating vegetables. It is well worth considering if doing fairly limited cooking for one or two people; it takes up less room and is easier to clean than a food processor.

Saucepans   Two or three sizes of thick-bottomed saucepans, depending on the number you are cooking for, plus one non-stick pan.

Frying Pans   A large and a small heavy frying pan. Non-stick surfaces are useful both in cooking and cleaning, but remember that they should not be used over a very high heat so they are not as good for searing meats, etc.

Blender   I have two blenders, a normal size one, and a small one which I find extremely useful because there are a number of tasks for which the other one is too large, such as making small quantities of mayonnaise or chopping herbs. For tasks such as puréeing I tend to use a blender rather than a food processor, as the results are often better and the blender is easier to wash up.

Food Processor   Food processors have their limitations; they reduce onions to a watery mass, and chopped meat to a paste almost in the blink of an eye. They make a sticky mess of pastry if not watched carefully all the time, cannot whisk egg whites, whip cream or purée potatoes and can be fiddly to wash up. Unless you have a model with a small bowl attachment they cannot cope with small quantities.

Steamer   This could simply be a metal fan-shaped, or petal, basket, a classic one that sits on a saucepan, or an electric one.

Slotted Spoon   For scooping foods cleanly from their cooking liquid.

Wooden Spoons   One with a square edge gets right into the corners.

Bristle Pastry Brush   For brushing foods with oil or melted butter prior to grilling.

WINE

Wine goes particularly well with French food. Gone are the days when it was felt necessary to adhere to strict rules governing what wine should be served with what food. Drink what you like is the current approach. Whilst convention could be restrictive, it did at least provide a novice with some guidance. Nowadays many of us spend a lot of time pondering the wine shelves of supermarkets or off-licences, wondering which wine to buy.

To gain the most enjoyment from both food and wine it is best to match their styles. In other words, serve a light wine, whether white or red, with a light dish, an inexpensive wine with a casual snack, a more expensive wine with a more formal dish. You can alter the emphasis of the 'weight' of a dish by your choice of wine, but you should still stay within the same broad style. For example, a medium-bodied white wine with lamb can make the dish seem lighter, more summery, than a fruity red wine.

If you find that a red wine tastes rather 'hard' or tannic, try pouring it into another bottle. This allows air to get to the wine and soften the taste.

It is unlikely that a heavy robust wine would be appropriate for any dish cooked quickly.

Unless you keep white wine in the refrigerator as a matter of course, or have thought about it in advance, having white wine sufficiently chilled when you want to drink it soon after getting in from work can be a problem. Instead of standing the bottle in the door of the fridge, lay it where it is coldest: on the top shelf if you have a fridge with an ice-making compartment, the bottom shelf if you don't. Or you can pop it in the freezer, providing you do not leave it there for too long. To continue chilling the bottle whilst it is on the table, slip it into a special 'sleeve' specifically designed for the purpose. It folds flat for keeping in the freezer or freezing compartment of the refrigerator until required.

Opposite: Pea and Lettuce Soup (page 4), Tomato and Basil Soup (page 2) and Grilled Goat's Cheese Croûtes (page 23)

Opposite page 1: Tapenade (page 21), Anchöiade (page 20) and Eggs Poached on Mediterranean Vegetables (page 15)

CHAPTER ONE

FIRST COURSES & LIGHT MEALS

THIS SECTION contains a broad range of dishes because it can be difficult to categorise recipes precisely. What on one occasion is a first course can just as well serve as a snack at another time – for example, soups can be the start of a large meal, or can make a light meal on their own if served in larger portions, accompanied by good country bread, and followed by cheese with the bread, then fruit.

I have always used stock if at all possible for soups, as it gives body and depth to the flavour. But since experimenting with making soups quickly I have discovered that the need for stock can be reduced by simply adding more vegetables and herbs to strengthen the flavour.

· TOMATO AND BASIL SOUP ·

MADE from well-flavoured tomatoes, this soup has everything in its favour – flavour, simplicity and speed. The tomatoes stew gently in their own juice, so their full, glorious summer flavour is retained. If there is time, lightly chill the soup before serving with French bread.

SERVES 4

1kg (2lb) well-flavoured tomatoes, including stalks, halved
2 red peppers, seeded and chopped (optional)
575ml (1 pint) vegetable stock or 300ml (½ pint) each vegetable stock (or water) and medium-bodied dry white wine

several sprigs of basil
salt and freshly ground black pepper

1. Put the tomatoes, peppers if using, the stock or water, and wine if using, in a saucepan. Bring to the boil, then simmer, uncovered, for about 10 minutes.

2. Meanwhile, shred the basil leaves.

3. Purée the soup briefly in a food processor or blender, then pass through a sieve into the saucepan. Add the basil and seasoning and reheat. Serve accompanied by French bread.

· CAULIFLOWER AND ALMOND SOUP ·

IN MY house this is known as 'the mistress' soup' because, in France, dishes or garnishes containing cauliflower are dedicated to Madame du Barry, mistress of Louis XV. Add a large knob of butter, or some soft cheese, in place of some of the milk, but do not boil it – just stir it in and heat through at the end of the cooking.

SERVES 4

875ml (1½ pints) vegetable, chicken or veal stock
1 medium cauliflower
75g (3oz) flaked almonds
6 spring onions

1 bay leaf
225ml (8fl oz) milk
salt and freshly ground black pepper

1. Bring 575ml (1 pint) of the stock to the boil. Meanwhile, divide the cauliflower into sprigs and chop them. Add the cauliflower and half the almonds to the stock and leave to simmer, uncovered, while you chop the white part of the spring onions. Add these to the pan with the bay leaf and continue to simmer until the cauliflower is tender.

2. Preheat the grill. Spread the remaining almonds in a single layer in a shallow baking dish and toast, stirring occasionally, until they are an even light brown.

3. Remove the bay leaf. Purée the soup, return to the pan and add the remaining stock. Boil for about 3 minutes, then add the milk. Heat through and season. Serve with the toasted almonds scattered over.

VARIATION

Omit the almonds and serve the soup with Grilled Goat's Cheese Croûtes (see page 23) floating on top.

· PEA AND LETTUCE SOUP ·

THE French name for this delicate soup is *Potage Saint-Germain*, because, for some obscure reason, dishes including peas bear the name of Comte de Saint-Germain, Louis XV's war minister. For a delicate soup tasting just of the sweet flavour of peas, use only a light stock – vegetable is best – or half stock and half water; alternatively this is an occasion when you can get away with all water. A handful of peas can be cooked or heated separately to use for garnishing the soup.

SERVES 4

55g (2oz) unsalted butter
1 leek
1 small round lettuce
about 875ml (1½ pints) vegetable or
 chicken stock, or water
several sprigs of chervil

a few sprigs of parsley
450g (1lb) fresh or frozen peas
salt and freshly ground black
 pepper
cream (optional)

1. Melt the butter in a saucepan. Slice the leek and cook until softened but not coloured.

2. Meanwhile, divide the lettuce into leaves and stir into the pan until they wilt. Add the stock or water, chervil, parsley and fresh peas if using, bring to the boil and simmer for 10 minutes. Add frozen peas, if using, quickly return to the boil, then simmer until tender.

3. Purée the soup in a food processor or blender, then pour back into the pan, reheat and season to taste. If the soup is too thick, add some boiling stock or water. Serve with a little cream swirled through, if liked.

· CHUNKY LENTIL AND HERB SOUP ·

THIS soup is suitable for a light meal (it is also my favourite for taking in a vacuum flask as part of a packed lunch on cold days). The vegetables and herbs can be varied according to what is available. And for vegetarians the lardons or bacon can be replaced by chestnut (brown) mushrooms.

SERVES 4

2 tablespoons olive oil
1 onion, chopped
2 cloves garlic, chopped
115g (4oz) lardons or diced thick-cut streaky bacon
1 leek
2 carrots
1 stick of celery
175g (6oz) green or brown lentils

400g (14oz) passata
a handful of herbs such as parsley, tarragon, thyme, marjoram
1 bay leaf, torn
salt and freshly ground black pepper
Cheese, Garlic or Plain Croûtons (see page 10)
chopped parsley

1. Heat the oil in a saucepan, add the onion, garlic and bacon and fry for 4–5 minutes.

2. Meanwhile, chop the leek, carrots and celery. Stir the chopped vegetables into the pan with the lentils, passata, herbs and 900ml (1½ pints) water. Bring to the boil, then simmer until the vegetables and lentils are tender (about 25 minutes, depending on the lentils).

3. Season the soup and serve garnished with croûtons and chopped parsley.

· LEEK AND POTATO SOUP ·

POTATOES become gluey if puréed in a food processor or blender so, unless I have time to press the vegetables through a food mill or sieve, I leave the soup chunky.

SERVES 4

---

3 large leeks, sliced
55g (2oz) unsalted butter
350g (12oz) potatoes
875ml (1½ pints) chicken, veal or
   vegetable stock

salt and freshly ground black
   pepper
crème fraîche, whipping cream,
   fromage frais or soft cheese
   (optional)
chopped parsley

---

1. Gently cook the leeks in the butter until softened but not coloured.

2. Meanwhile, chop the potatoes into fairly small pieces, stir into the leeks for 2–3 minutes, then add the stock and bring to the boil. Simmer gently until the vegetables are tender.

3. Season to taste, remove the pan from the heat, and add a swirl of crème fraîche, whipping cream, fromage frais or soft cheese if liked, then sprinkle with chopped parsley. Serve with wholemeal, Granary or herb bread.

· WATERCRESS SOUP ·

For a creamier soup, milk can be substituted for half the stock; or 2 egg yolks blended with 2–3 spoonfuls crème fraîche or cream can be stirred into the soup after puréeing, heated gently and stirred until thickened. I like to stir a dollop of soft cheese into each bowl of soup; a small nut of butter, or a swirl of cream or thick plain yogurt can be added if preferred.

SERVES 4 AS A FIRST COURSE, 3 FOR A SNACK OR LIGHT MEAL

25g (1oz) unsalted butter
2 onions, chopped
225g (½lb) old potatoes, chopped
875ml (1½ pints) vegetable or
chicken stock, or water
2 bunches watercress, about 225g
(½lb)

salt and freshly ground black
pepper
Plain or Cheese Croûtons (see page
10)
chopped chives (optional)

1. Heat the butter in a saucepan, add the onions and potatoes and stir for about 2 minutes to coat well with butter. Add the stock or water, and bring to the boil. Then simmer, uncovered, for about 15 minutes, depending on the size of the pieces of potato, until tender.

2. Meanwhile, remove the tough stalks from the watercress. Stir the watercress sprigs into the soup and simmer for 1 minute.

3. Very briefly purée the soup in a food processor or blender, then pour back into the pan and reheat. Season, and adjust the thickness if necessary by adding a little boiling stock or water. Serve garnished with croûtons and chopped chives, if liked.

· MUSHROOM SOUP ·

THIS is a really mushroom-packed soup that can be made with water instead of stock. You can use milk or cream in place of some of the water, but it's best to add it at the end of cooking and just heat it through, to avoid a 'boiled milk' taste.

SERVES 4

40g (1½oz) unsalted butter
3 shallots, chopped
2 cloves garlic, crushed
675g (1½lb) chestnut (brown)
  mushrooms
575ml (1 pint) chicken, vegetable or
  veal stock, or water
1 tablespoon wholegrain mustard

salt and freshly ground black
  pepper
crème fraîche or whipping cream,
  or fromage frais or soft cheese
  (optional)
Garlic or Plain Croûtons (see page
  10)

1. Heat the butter in a saucepan, add the shallots and garlic and cook gently until softened.

2. Meanwhile, roughly slice or chop the mushrooms, then add to the pan and cook, stirring occasionally, for a few minutes.

3. Pour the stock or water into the pan, bring to the boil, then simmer for about 15 minutes.

4. If liked, tip the contents of the pan into a blender or food processor and process briefly, leaving some texture.

5. Return the soup to the pan, stir in the mustard and seasoning and reheat gently.

6. Swirl through some crème fraîche or whipping cream, or add a dollop of fromage frais or soft cheese, if liked. Serve with croûtons scattered over.

· COURGETTE AND LETTUCE SOUP ·

A SIMPLE, light soup that is perfect for summer. If you plan ahead, it is equally good, if not better, eaten lightly chilled.

SERVES 4

25g (1oz) unsalted butter, diced
1 onion
550g (1¼lb) small courgettes
1 round lettuce
800ml (27fl oz) vegetable stock

2–3 tablespoons fromage frais
salt and freshly ground black
 pepper
chopped chervil or parsley

1. Heat the butter in a saucepan. Meanwhile, finely chop the onion, then cook until translucent while thinly slicing the courgettes. Stir them into the pan and leave to cook over a low heat while you tear the lettuce leaves into pieces. Add these to the pan with a little of the stock and cook for 1–2 minutes until the lettuce has wilted but retains its colour.

2. Tip the contents of the pan into a blender, add half the stock and fromage frais and blend until smooth.

3. Return the soup to the pan, stir in the remaining stock and the seasoning and heat through without boiling. Swirl through the remaining fromage frais and serve sprinkled with chopped chervil or parsley.

· CROÛTONS ·

CROÛTONS can be used to accompany soups, in salads of bitter leaves (such as curly endive, spinach and watercress), and as an omelette filling. Croûtons can also be made from fried bread, but this requires more attention, and more oil, so the croûtons are not as dry and light. If you have some spare bread when you have the oven on, bake some slices until crisp and hardly coloured (the time will depend on the temperature of the oven), coat with oil as below and return to the oven until golden. You can store Croûtons in a plastic bag in the refrigerator for several days.

about ¾–1 slice firm day-old bread
   per person
1 clove garlic (optional)
olive oil

salt and freshly ground black
   pepper
freshly grated Parmesan or finely
   chopped herbs (optional)

1. Preheat the grill to moderate. Remove the crusts from the bread and halve the garlic clove if used. Pour the olive oil over the centre of a plate.

2. Toast both sides of the bread until crisp but hardly coloured. Rub the bread with the garlic, if used, as thoroughly as you like. Then lay each side of the bread on the oil to coat lightly, adding more oil if necessary.

3. Season lightly and return the bread to the grill until golden.

4. Cut into cubes and toss with the Parmesan or herbs, if using.

· OMELETTE AUX FINES HERBES ·

THIS classic omelette, consisting simply of fresh farm eggs and a mixture of chopped chervil, parsley, tarragon and chives, is often overlooked but is hard to beat. The keys to success are using fresh free-range eggs and cooking the omelette correctly so it is still moist and creamy on top.

SERVES 1

3 eggs
salt and freshly ground black
  pepper
15g (½oz) unsalted butter, diced

scant tablespoon finely chopped
  mixed chervil, parsley, tarragon
  and chives

1. Beat the eggs together lightly with a fork, then mix in the seasoning.

2. Heat the butter in a 15–18cm (6–7 inch) omelette pan, or frying pan. Pour in the eggs and swirl the pan once or twice. At the same time stir with a fork, bringing the cooking egg from the side of the pan to the centre, and allowing liquid egg to run on to the surface of the pan. Repeat two or three times. Then leave the omelette to cook for a short while longer until the underside is set and lightly golden and the top still moist and creamy.

3. Sprinkle over the herbs, lift the pan so the edge of the omelette near the handle flops over (help it with a fork, if necessary) and roll it down the pan on to a waiting warm plate.

VARIATIONS

1. For Asparagus Omelette, omit the herbs. Thinly slice 12 thin asparagus spears on the diagonal, then put to fry gently in 25g (1oz) unsalted butter until tender while you make the omelette. Add the asparagus when you finish stirring.

2. Other quick ideas for omelettes include creamy blue cheese, such as Fourme d'Ambert, and walnuts; broad beans with goat's cheese or prawns; and quartered artichokes in oil, with parsley.

· BAKED EGGS WITH SPINACH IN BRIOCHES ·

THE scooped out centres of the brioches can be made into crumbs for another recipe where breadcrumbs are called for.

--- SERVES 2 ---

25–40g (1–1½oz) unsalted butter
a small handful of spinach leaves,
    stalks removed, shredded
4 individual, approximately 3½oz
    (100g), brioches
nutmeg

salt and freshly ground black
    pepper
4 small eggs
about 15g (½oz) Gruyère cheese,
    grated

1. Preheat the oven to 200°C/400°F/Gas Mark 6 and place a baking sheet in the oven to heat.

2. Heat a small knob of about 15g (½oz) butter in a small frying pan and add the shredded spinach. Sir for a few minutes until the spinach has wilted and the surplus water has evaporated. Tip into a colander and squeeze out as much water as possible.

3. Break off and reserve the brioche topknots. Then, using a teaspoon, carefully scoop out the crumbs from the brioches to leave four shells; do not pierce the walls.

4. Divide the spinach mixture between the brioches and season with a fine grating of nutmeg, and salt and pepper. Place on the baking sheet.

5. Carefully break an egg into each brioche shell, sprinkle with cheese, add the remaining butter, and pepper. Bake for about 10 minutes, then put the reserved brioche topknots on the baking sheet and cook for a further 5 minutes or so until the eggs are cooked to the required degree.

6. Replace the topknots on the brioches and serve.

· BAKED EGGS EN COCOTTE ·

IN THEIR simplest (but nevertheless delicious) form eggs baked in small dishes are moistened with a little butter, crème fraîche or cream and lightly flavoured with a herb such as tarragon. But they can easily be glamorised by adding diced raw or cooked ham, sautéed mushrooms, spinach purée flavoured with a hint of nutmeg and a little grated cheese, watercress and bacon, smoked salmon with soft cheese and chives, or a spoonful of artichoke cream or pesto beneath the egg and grated cheese sprinkled on top.

The eggs can also be cooked on the hob: put the dishes in a deep frying pan, pour in boiling water to come three-quarters of the way up the sides, cover with a lid or foil, then cook gently with the water barely bubbling.

SERVES 4

6 tablespoons crème fraîche, or single or double cream
1 tablespoon chopped tarragon

salt and freshly ground black pepper
4 eggs

1. Preheat the oven to 180°C/350°F/Gas Mark 4. Generously butter four ramekin dishes and put them in a baking dish. Bring a kettle of water to the boil.

2. Mix the crème fraîche or cream with the tarragon and seasoning, then divide half between the dishes.

3. Break an egg into each dish and spoon over the remaining crème fraîche or cream. Pour enough boiling water around the dishes to come halfway up the sides, then bake for about 10 minutes or until the eggs are cooked to your liking.

· HERB CUSTARDS ·

IF THERE is time, gently heat the herbs in the milk and cream, then cover, remove from the heat and leave to infuse for up to 30 minutes. The custards can also be steamed (lay a sheet of greaseproof paper over the dishes before putting the lid on the steaming basket) or cooked in a deep frying pan surrounded by barely simmering water. If you are not bothered about turning out the custards they can be eaten, with spoons, from the dishes as soon as they are cooked.

SERVES 2–3

4 eggs
115ml (4fl oz) milk
4 tablespoons double or whipping
  cream
4 tablespoons chopped herbs such
  as parsley, basil, thyme,
  marjoram, tarragon, chives

4 teaspoons freshly grated
  Parmesan cheese
salt and freshly ground black
  pepper

---

1. Preheat the oven to 180°C/350°F/Gas Mark 4. Butter two or three ramekin dishes and place in a roasting or baking tin.

2. Lightly beat the eggs with a fork, and stir in the milk, cream, herbs, cheese and seasoning. Pour into the dishes, then pour enough boiling water around the dishes to come halfway up the sides. Bake for about 20 minutes or until just set in the centre.

3. Remove the dishes from the roasting tin and allow the eggs to stand for a few minutes. Then run the point of a sharp knife round the edge of each custard and invert on to warm plates. Serve with thin buttered toast.

· Eggs Poached on Mediterranean Vegetables ·

A SUBSTANTIAL snack, first course, or light lunch or supper if served with country bread, this is not only quick, but uses only one pan for cooking and no serving dish. If you would like a smarter presentation, as you might for a first course, you could transfer the vegetables to a large shallow baking dish, or four individual dishes, then add the eggs.

I sometimes scatter about 125g (4oz) grated Gruyère cheese, or crumbled goat's cheese, over the eggs just after they have been added; if using the former I place the pan under a preheated grill for about 7 minutes or until the eggs are just set and the cheese bubbling.

SERVES 4

2 tablespoons olive oil	4 well-flavoured tomatoes
½ large onion	2 teaspoons chopped rosemary
1 red pepper	salt and freshly ground black
175g (6oz) small courgettes	pepper
1–2 cloves garlic	4 eggs

1. Heat the oil in a large frying pan. Meanwhile, thinly slice the onion and add to the pan, while you core, seed and chop the red pepper. Stir the pepper into the pan, then slice the courgettes and stir into the other vegetables. Cook until beginning to soften, stirring occasionally.

2. Crush the garlic, and seed and chop the tomatoes, then stir into the pan with the rosemary and seasoning. Cook, stirring occasionally, until the vegetables are tender.

3. Make four slight hollows in the vegetable mixture with the back of a spoon, then break an egg carefully into each hollow. Season, cover the pan and cook gently for about 5 minutes for creamy yolks, longer if you prefer the eggs more well-cooked.

· POACHED EGGS ON GRILLED FIELD MUSHROOMS ·

POACHED Eggs on Grilled Field Mushrooms is high on my list of favourite snacks or light meals. As with Spinach and Poached Egg Salad (see page 35), it is much nicer if you cook the egg lightly so that the yolk forms a sauce when it is cut.

The recipe below is the basic one which I frequently vary according to what is available and how desperate I am to eat. For example, I sometimes fry the mushrooms stalks with chopped shallots or spring onions and, perhaps, garlic, bacon or ham; and I sometimes include well-drained cooked spinach. Or I may simply brush the mushroom caps with melted butter, or oil, then place a nut of soft, ordinary or goat's cheese beneath the eggs. All the herbs can be varied, and you can use fresh (rather than toasted) bread if you wish.

SERVES 4

4 large open field mushrooms
2 tablespoons chopped parsley,
　　tarragon and thyme
unsalted butter
salt and freshly ground black
　　pepper

4 eggs
4 slices firm country, granary or
　　wholemeal bread
a few chives, chopped

---

1. Preheat the grill. Remove the stalks from the mushrooms, chop finely and mix with the herbs. Divide between the mushroom caps and place a dot of butter on each. Season the mushrooms, then grill for 5–7 minutes.

2. Meanwhile, bring a frying pan of water to just on simmering point. Carefully break one egg at a time into the water. Baste the yolks with water, then cover and leave for about 3 minutes until the yolks have a white covering.

3. Toast the bread, alongside the mushrooms or in the toaster.

4. Butter the toast and place a mushroom on each slice. Remove the eggs from the water using a slotted spoon, then place on the mushrooms. Sprinkle with chives and season, using plenty of black pepper, and serve immediately.

VARIATION

Baked Eggs on Mushrooms

1. Place the mushroom caps in individual dishes. Preheat the oven to 200°C/400°F/Gas Mark 6.

2. Fry the chopped stalks, if liked, with chopped spring onions or shallots, then divide between the mushroom caps.

3. Break an egg on to each cap, sprinkle with chopped chives, parsley or tarragon, then trickle over a little cream.

4. Bake for 10–15 minutes.

· SCRAMBLED EGGS WITH PRAWNS, ON TOAST ·

SCRAMBLED eggs need to be cooked gently if they are to be soft, creamy and barely set. As the eggs continue to cook in their own heat, you should remove the pan from the stove just before the mixture is ready.

Chestnut (otherwise known as brown), oyster, shiitake or wild mushrooms, grated Gruyère cheese and chives, and creamed spinach are also very good with scrambled eggs, but do not use so much of any flavouring that it swamps the eggs.

SERVES 2

knob of unsalted butter, plus extra
   for toast
4 eggs
2 slices wholemeal bread
about 40g (1½oz) large peeled
   prawns, chopped
1½ tablespoons cream, fromage
   frais or milk

2 teaspoons chopped tarragon,
   chives or 2–3 teaspoons chopped
   watercress leaves
salt and freshly ground black
   pepper

---

1. Heat the butter in a heavy, preferably non-stick, saucepan. Lightly beat the eggs.

2. Toast the bread. Meanwhile, swirl the butter around the pan, pour in the eggs and cook very gently, stirring almost constantly with a wooden spoon, until the eggs are just beginning to become very lightly set.

3. Stir the prawns into the eggs for a few more moments. Then remove from the heat and stir in the cream, fromage frais or milk, the herbs and the seasoning.

4. Butter the toast, then spoon on the scrambled eggs and serve.

· MUSHROOMS ON TOAST ·

MEATY mushrooms in a light creamy herb sauce, served on good thick toast that soaks up the savoury juices, make about the quickest and most satisfying snack I know. To make a dish substantial enough for a light meal, add chopped shallot and/or diced bacon.

There is no need to peel mushrooms, and they certainly should not be washed (like sponges, they soak up water). If the mushrooms are dirty, wipe them with a damp cloth.

SERVES 2

25g (1oz) unsalted butter
1 clove garlic, crushed
250g (9oz) open or large cap
  chestnut (brown) mushrooms
2 thick slices firm bread
juice of ½ lemon

2 tablespoons chopped parsley or
  tarragon
salt and freshly ground black
  pepper
¼–½ teaspoon Dijon mustard
1½–2 tablespoons fromage frais,
  crème fraîche or soft cheese

1. Preheat the grill for the toast. Heat the butter in a frying pan, add the garlic and cook until the butter becomes fragrant.

2. Meanwhile, clean the mushrooms, if necessary, and cut into quarters.

3. Remove the garlic from the pan. Then add the mushrooms and cook over a fairly high heat, shaking the pan occasionally, until the mushrooms have almost cooked to the required degree and the moisture has evaporated.

4. Meanwhile, toast the bread on both sides.

5. Add some lemon juice, the parsley or tarragon, and seasoning to the mushrooms and cook gently, while you stir the mustard into the fromage frais, crème fraîche or soft cheese. Stir this mixture into the pan, bubble to thicken if necessary, then pile the mushrooms and juices on to the hot toast and serve.

· Anchoïade and Tapenade ·

ANCHOÏADE and Tapenade are two essential pastes used in Provençal cooking. Anchoïade has, as the name suggests, an anchovy base, while Tapenade contains capers and black olives. But they have a number of similarities – both are made by pounding the ingredients together, both are pungent, and can be kept in a tightly covered jar in the refrigerator for several weeks (although they should be served at room temperature rather than chilled).

They can also both be used in similar ways for quick first courses or snacks, or livening up main courses: spread on country bread (fresh, toasted or baked), then top with sliced tomatoes; spread on wholemeal toast, then top with scrambled eggs or soft cheese sprinkled with chopped chives; mix with the yolk for a filling for hard-boiled eggs; or serve as a dip with crudités. Anchoïade can also be spread on lamb or served with grilled salmon; while grilled pork chops can be topped with a small spoonful of Tapenade.

ANCHOÏADE

2 cloves garlic
20 anchovy fillets, rinsed if
    necessary
about 1½ tablespoons torn basil
5 tablespoons virgin olive oil

2–3 teaspoons red wine vinegar
2 teaspoons tomato purée,
    preferably sun-dried (optional)
freshly ground black pepper

1. Mix the garlic and anchovy fillets together in a small blender or food processor. Add the basil. Then, with the motor running, very slowly pour in the olive oil.

2. Mix in the vinegar and tomato purée, if using, and season with pepper. Keep in a covered glass jar in the refrigerator.

3. Stir and adjust the level of vinegar and basil before serving.

TAPENADE

200g (7oz) oil-cured black olives,
preferably Nyons or another small
black variety, pitted
55g (2oz) capers, preferably dry
salt packed
4 anchovy fillets, rinsed if necessary
1–2 cloves garlic

115ml (4fl oz) olive oil
1 tablespoon Dijon mustard
1 teaspoon chopped thyme
lemon juice
freshly ground black pepper

1. Mix the olives, capers, anchovies and garlic to a paste in a small blender or food processor. With the motor running, very slowly pour in the oil to make a paste.

2. Mix in the mustard, thyme, lemon juice to taste and plenty of black pepper. Adjust the consistency (it should be a thick, spreadable paste) and pungency, adding more oil to mellow it if necessary.

3. Keep in a covered glass jar in the refrigerator.

· CHICKEN LIVERS ON TOAST ·

COOK the chicken livers quickly so the outside becomes crisp but the inside remains soft and pink. In this recipe capers, bacon and red wine add a savoury piquancy. To complete the dish, serve on toasted firm country bread which absorbs the rich juices.

SERVES 2

45g (1½oz) lardons or cubes of
  thick-cut streaky bacon
1 shallot
25g (1oz) unsalted butter
225g (½lb) chicken livers
5 tablespoons red wine

2 teaspoons capers
salt and freshly ground black
  pepper
lemon juice (optional)
chopped parsley or tarragon

---

1. Heat the lardons or bacon cubes in a frying pan until the fat runs.

2. Meanwhile, chop the shallot. Add the butter to the pan. When it has melted add the chopped shallot and cook until soft.

3. Stir the chicken livers into the pan, cook quickly for 1–1½ minutes until crisp on the outside and still pink in the centre. Using a slotted spoon, transfer the chicken livers to a warm plate, cover and keep warm.

4. Stir the wine into the pan, dislodging the sediment, and boil briskly until slightly reduced. Add the capers and return the chicken livers, and any juices collected on the plate, to the pan. Season and add a squeeze of lemon juice, if liked. Serve sprinkled with chopped parsley or tarragon.

VARIATION

Chicken Livers with Grapes

1. Omit the bacon, shallot and capers and replace the red wine with 6 tablespoons medium-bodied dry white wine.

2. Fry the chicken livers in 50g (2oz) unsalted butter as above, remove and keep warm.

3. Boil the white wine until slightly reduced, then add 125g (4oz) halved seedless white grapes. Heat through, and add the cooked livers, seasoning and any herbs.

· GRILLED GOAT'S CHEESE CROÛTES ·

IF YOU prefer, you can put all the cheese on one larger slice of bread. Pesto or sun-dried tomato paste can be spread on the toast before the cheese is added. The Croûtes can be eaten as they are, or on a crisp green salad. They can also be floated on vegetable soups such as Cauliflower, made without almonds (page 3), or Leek and Potato (page 6).

SERVES 1

4 fairly thin slices French *ficelle* (stick), Granary or wholemeal bread
1 goat's cheese weighing about 115g (4oz)

olive oil
freshly ground black pepper
1 good sprig of thyme (optional)

1. Preheat the grill.

2. Toast the bread on one side until crisp and golden.

3. Meanwhile, slice the cheese horizontally.

4. Brush the untoasted sides of the bread lightly with olive oil, then place the cheese on top. Sprinkle with black pepper, and thyme leaves, if used, then return to the grill for about 3 minutes.

· PEAR AND BLUE CHEESE ON TOAST ·

A CREAMY Bleu d'Auvergne, Fourme d'Ambert or Bresse Bleu will melt readily to collapse over the pear. Serve with a small (undressed) tomato and watercress salad, well seasoned with black pepper.

SERVES 2

2 thick slices wholegrain bread
1 ripe pear
about 75g (3oz) blue cheese

unsalted butter
wholegrain mustard
freshly ground black pepper

1. Preheat the grill, then toast the bread on one side.

2. Meanwhile, peel, halve, core and slice the pear, and slice the cheese.

3. Spread the untoasted sides of the bread with butter and a little mustard, then arrange the pear slices on top. Cover with slices of cheese, grind over some black pepper, and place under the grill until the cheese oozes around the pear.

VARIATION

Alternatively, simply mash good Roquefort on hot brown toast.

· CROQUE MONSIEUR ·

I WONDER why a toasted or fried ham and cheese sandwich should be for a man to munch (*croquer* means 'to munch'). Frying produces a crisper, crunchier sandwich, but I prefer the drier, less rich result gained by toasting. Add slices of tomato and/or chopped herbs, such as chives, basil or tarragon, if you have them.

SERVES 2

4 slices firm bread
unsalted butter
55g (2oz) Gruyère cheese, grated

2 slices ham
mustard

1. Preheat the grill.

2. Butter each slice of bread on one side. Sprinkle half the grated cheese over the buttered sides of two slices, top each with a slice of ham and spread with a little mustard. Cover the ham with the remaining cheese, put the remaining bread on top, buttered side down, and press together.

3. Grill the sandwiches on both sides until the bread is toasted and the cheese melted.

· GRILLED CHICORY WITH WALNUTS AND CHEESE ·

THE cheese should be a soft one so that it begins to melt when it comes into contact with the hot chicory.

———— SERVES 2 ————

4 heads of chicory
virgin olive oil or walnut oil
freshly ground black pepper
about 1½–2 tablespoons chopped
    walnuts

2–3oz (50–75g) soft goat's cheese
    or creamy blue cheese such as
    Fourme d'Ambert

1. Preheat the grill. Cut the chicory in half lengthways, brush with olive or walnut oil, sprinkle with black pepper and arrange in a heatproof dish.

2. Grill the chicory for a few minutes, turning and basting with oil once or twice until it is soft in the centre and the edges are charred in patches. About three-quarters of the way through cooking, sprinkle over the chopped nuts so they become crisp but do not burn.

3. Meanwhile, cut the cheese into small pieces.

4. Scatter the cheese over the hot chicory and return to the grill briefly, if necessary, so the cheese just begins to melt. Trickle over a little more virgin olive oil or walnut oil and serve immediately.

· DEEP-FRIED CAMEMBERT ·

WITH a crisp coating holding in oozing molten cheese, deep-fried Camembert was an old favourite a few years ago on restaurant menus where it would invariably be accompanied by some form of sweet fruit purée or compote, which never did appeal to me. A crisp green salad seems far more appropriate. If you do not have a deep-fryer, cook the cheeses in an ordinary medium-sized saucepan and use a slotted spoon for lowering them into and taking them out of the pan.

SERVES 2

55–75g (2–3oz) fine fresh
   breadcrumbs or a mixture of
   breadcrumbs and fine cornmeal
   or fine oats
freshly ground black pepper

1 whole Camembert, cut into
   6 triangles
1 egg, beaten
olive oil
crisp salad

1. Season the breadcrumbs, or mixture of breadcrumbs and fine cornmeal or fine oats, with black pepper.

2. Dip the Camembert in beaten egg, then in the seasoned breadcrumbs. Repeat if necessary to give a good covering.

3. Place the cheese in the freezer or refrigerator while heating a deep-fryer or saucepan half-filled with oil to 180°C (350°F), or until a cube of stale bread browns in 1 minute.

4. Add the cheese to the oil and fry for 2–3 minutes until lightly browned. Remove the cheese from the oil with a slotted spoon, drain quickly on paper towels, and serve immediately with a crisp green salad.

· ASPARAGUS WITH QUICK HOLLANDAISE SAUCE ·

WHEREAS we prefer our own green asparagus, in France fatter, blanched white asparagus is more popular. It probably comes down to favouring not only what is familiar, but also, in the case of asparagus, what is freshest (asparagus deteriorates very quickly after harvesting).

The making of Hollandaise Sauce used to be viewed with awe and trepidation, but with a blender it is quick and easy. Hollandaise also goes well with broccoli, boiled or steamed potatoes and grilled fish.

Steaming asparagus keeps it dry and eliminates having to leave it on wads of paper towels to drain or else risk the juice running up your arms as you eat the spears – with your fingers, of course.

SERVES 4

550g (1¼lb) asparagus

Quick Hollandaise sauce
about 150g (5oz) unsalted butter, diced
about 1 tablespoon lemon juice
1 large egg yolk
salt and freshly ground black pepper

---

1. Bring the base of a steamer, or a saucepan, about a quarter filled with water, to the boil. Trim the asparagus and put the spears in a steaming basket. Cover and put to steam for about 10–12 minutes.

2. Meanwhile, to make the sauce, gently heat the butter until melted but not too hot. In another small saucepan, warm the lemon juice.

3. Put the egg yolk into a blender, add the lemon juice and blend. With the motor running, slowly pour in the melted butter until the sauce thickens. Season and add more lemon juice if necessary.

4. Transfer the asparagus to warm plates and spoon some of the sauce to the side, or serve it separately.

· BROAD BEANS AND ARTICHOKES ·

Bayonne ham, which is produced in the Pyrenees, has a unique flavour resulting from the wine that is used during the curing. It is delicious eaten raw, or added to quickly cooked dishes. If you are unable to find Bayonne ham, use Parma ham instead. Serve with a main course that will not require attention at the same time, such as Baked Chicken with Rosemary (see page 72), Fish Parcels with Herbs (see page 50), or Steak with Herb Sauce (see page 60).

SERVES 4

350g (12oz) shelled fresh or frozen broad beans
4–5 spring onions
2 small cloves garlic
1½ tablespoons oil from the jar of artichokes
three-quarters of a 400g (14oz) jar artichokes in oil
1 bay leaf

3 tablespoons medium-bodied dry white wine
55g (2oz) raw ham such as Bayonne
3 tablespoons chopped parsley
a squeeze of lemon juice
salt and freshly ground black pepper

1. Cook the beans in boiling salted water until just tender, then drain.

2. Meanwhile, chop the spring onions and crush the garlic.

3. Heat the artichoke oil in a large frying pan, add the spring onion and garlic and fry until softened and lightly coloured.

4. Meanwhile, halve the artichokes, then stir into the pan with the beans, bay leaf, wine and 3–4 tablespoons water. Cover and cook for about 3 minutes, shaking the pan occasionally.

5. Chop the ham and add to the pan with the parsley, lemon juice and seasoning. Cook, uncovered, for 2–3 minutes, and serve.

· LEEKS VINAIGRETTE ·

LEEKS Vinaigrette, served warm, bathed in a pungent mustard dressing are a favourite bistro dish. When boiled, leeks can become waterlogged and always need to be dried on pads of paper towels if they are not to dilute the dressing. I therefore take the easy option of steaming them. Chopped hard-boiled egg can be added to the parsley garnish if you wish.

SERVES 4

12 slim leeks, or 8 slightly larger ones
finely chopped parsley

Dressing
1 tablespoon white wine vinegar
1 tablespoon lemon juice

finely grated rind and juice of ½ orange
1 teaspoon Dijon mustard
4 tablespoons olive oil
salt and freshly ground black pepper

1. Steam the leeks in a single layer in a covered steaming basket for about 6–10 minutes, or until tender.

2. Meanwhile, warm a serving dish. Whisk together the vinegar, lemon and orange juices and mustard, then slowly pour in the oil, whisking constantly. Whisk in the orange rind and seasoning.

3. Transfer the leeks to the dish and gently stir in the dressing. If possible, leave to cool slightly. Serve sprinkled with parsley.

· HOT CHICK PEA SALAD ·

Mix the chick peas with the dressing while they are still as hot as possible, to create an immediate explosion of exciting aromas as the cold olive oil, herbs and mustard come into contact with the hot chick peas.

SERVES 4

2 × 400g (14oz) cans chick peas, drained and rinsed
2 plump cloves garlic
5 spring onions
1¼ tablespoons good-quality red wine vinegar
2–3 teaspoons Dijon mustard
salt and freshly ground black pepper

5 tablespoons fruity virgin or extra virgin olive oil
1½ tablespoons finely chopped parsley
1½ teaspoons finely chopped tarragon
extra chopped parsley

1. Put the chick peas in a saucepan with enough water just to cover them and slowly bring to the boil.

2. Meanwhile, finely chop the garlic and spring onions, keeping them separate.

3. Mix the garlic with the vinegar, mustard and seasoning, then slowly pour in the oil, whisking constantly.

4. Quickly drain the chick peas and immediately toss with the dressing, herbs and spring onions. Sprinkle with more chopped parsley and serve warm.

· CELERIAC RÉMOULADE ·

USUALLY *rémoulade* refers to mayonnaise flavoured with mustard, capers, gherkins, tarragon and sometimes anchovies, but when applied to celeriac, mustard is usually the only flavouring. You can, of course, add any or all of the other flavourings if you like, or some chopped walnuts. For a lighter sauce, substitute crème fraîche or thick yogurt for some of the mayonnaise. A food processor will make light work of grating celeriac; without one it's a little more laborious.

SERVES 4

150ml (¼ pint) mayonnaise
2–3 teaspoons Dijon mustard
lemon juice
450g (1lb) celeriac

salt and freshly ground black
   pepper
chopped chervil or parsley
lettuce leaves

1. Flavour the mayonnaise with mustard and lemon juice to taste; it should be quite 'mustardy'.

2. Bring a large saucepan of water to the boil. Meanwhile, peel and grate the celeriac, and boil for 30–60 seconds; celeriac tastes better if given this brief blanching but it is not vital.

3. Tip into a colander and rinse under cold running water. Drain well, then mix into the mayonnaise. Season, and sprinkle generously with chervil or parsley. Serve on a bed of lettuce leaves.

Opposite: Salmon with Red Wine (page 54) served with tagliatelle and a Green Salad (page 39)

· CRAB AND CELERIAC SALAD ·

CELERIAC goes extremely well with shellfish, particularly crab. In this recipe mustard, lemon, tomatoes and watercress play invaluable supporting roles. If serving this salad as a first course, prepare it before you cook the rest of the meal. Then there will be time to chill it for a little while (in the freezer if it's not for too long). If serving the salad as a snack, chill it if there is time, but don't worry if there isn't. Try to use fresh rather than frozen crabmeat.

SERVES 4

175g (6oz) celeriac
3 tablespoons lemon juice
2 teaspoons wholegrain mustard
salt and freshly ground black
 pepper
2 small dressed crabs

350g (12oz) well-flavoured
 tomatoes
a large bunch of watercress
toasted thinly sliced brown country
 bread

1. Bring a saucepan of water to the boil while you peel and coarsely grate the celeriac. Boil the celeriac for 1 minute, then tip into a colander and rinse under cold running water.

2. Stir together the lemon juice, mustard and seasoning.

3. Transfer the celeriac to a bowl, stir in the lemon juice mixture, then stir in the crabmeat with a fork so it is broken up. Cover and chill for as long as time allows.

4. Seed and chop the tomatoes. Discard the coarse stems from the watercress, then arrange the leaves on four plates.

5. Spoon the crab mixture on to the watercress leaves, and scatter over the chopped tomato. Serve with thin brown toast.

Opposite: Mussels in a Creamy Herb Sauce (page 58)

· WARM CURLY ENDIVE AND BACON SALAD ·

THIS salad can be served with a main course, or as a first course or snack; in which case I suggest using smoked bacon.

SERVES 2

115g (4oz) lardons or diced thick-
  cut bacon
½ head curly endive
1½ tablespoons walnut oil
1½ teaspoons red wine vinegar

¼–½ teaspoon Dijon mustard
salt and freshly ground black
  pepper
Croûtons (see page 10, optional)

1. Fry the bacon in a small, preferably non-stick, frying pan until the fat runs. Then continue to fry, stirring occasionally, until the bacon is crisp and brown.

2. Meanwhile, line a salad bowl with the curly endive leaves. Stir the walnut oil, vinegar, mustard and seasoning into the pan, dislodging the sediment, and heat until bubbling.

3. Pour the contents of the pan over the endive, toss, adding the croûtons if liked, and serve straight away.

· SPINACH AND POACHED EGG SALAD ·

THE highlight of this salad is the way the soft egg yolks languidly flow on to the salad, bathing it in limpid sauce. So, if you cook the eggs until the yolks are hard you will miss the main point of including them.

If the eggs are cooked before the bacon and croûtons are ready, transfer them to cold water, using a slotted spoon, to stop them cooking further. You could use ready-prepared plain or garlic Croûtons (see page 10) which only need to be reheated in the bacon fat.

I prefer this salad for a snack or light meal rather than as a first course, but if you have large appetites to satisfy, you could begin a meal with it.

SERVES 2

225g (½lb) young spinach leaves
55g (2oz) lardons or diced thick-cut
  streaky bacon
1 large slice country bread, cut into
  cubes
2 eggs

4 tablespoons olive oil, plus extra
  for frying
1 tablespoon red wine vinegar
1 teaspoon Dijon mustard
salt and freshly ground black
  pepper

---

1. Divide the spinach leaves between two plates.

2. Fry the bacon in a small, preferably non-stick, frying pan until the fat runs. Then add the bread cubes and continue to fry, stirring occasionally, until the bacon and croûtons are crisp and brown, adding more oil as necessary. Remove with a slotted spoon and scatter over the salad leaves.

3. Meanwhile, heat a larger frying pan, or other wide shallow pan, of water to boiling point. Remove from the heat, gently lower in the eggs, cover and leave for about 3 minutes or until the yolks have a white covering.

4. Mix together the oil, vinegar, mustard and seasoning, and stir into the frying pan, dislodging the sediment. Bring to the boil, then trickle over the spinach. Place one egg on each plate, season and serve.

· WARM POTATO SALAD ·

THIS classic salad with its creamy dressing is delicious served on its own, or as an accompaniment to grilled or barbecued meat; I also like it with halved boiled eggs and cheese omelettes.

The French potatoes to use for salads are the small, smooth-skinned varieties such as La Ratte and Belle de Fontenay. Alternatively, you could try the currently popular English variety, Pink Fir Apple. Tossing the potatoes with the dressing while they are hot transforms them as they absorb the flavours and creaminess.

Possible modifications include adding chopped Spanish onion or spring onions, substituting parsley for the dill or chives, and adding chopped anchovy fillets.

SERVES 4

675g (1½lb) small new potatoes

Dressing
175g (6oz) fromage frais
4–5 tablespoons mayonnaise
1½–2 tablespoons wholegrain
  mustard

4 tablespoons chopped dill or
  chives
lemon juice
salt and freshly ground black
  pepper

---

1. Boil the potatoes in their skins in salted water for 10 minutes, or until tender.

2. Meanwhile, stir together the fomage frais, mayonnaise, mustard and dill or chives until evenly combined. Then add lemon juice and seasoning to taste; adjust the amount of mustard if necessary.

3. Tip the potatoes into a colander to drain, transfer to a large warm bowl and stir in the dressing to coat completely. Leave to cool a little before serving.

· LEAF SALAD WITH BLUE CHEESE AND WALNUTS ·

I LIKE to lightly toast the walnuts before chopping them to give extra depth to their flavour. As it stands, this recipe serves two as a light main course or snack lunch or supper. If you wish to serve it as a side salad, slightly reduce the amount of cheese and nuts and use white wine vinegar instead of red.

SERVES 2-4

salad leaves such as watercress, rocket, spinach, curly endive or chicory
55g (2oz) walnuts, toasted if liked, roughly chopped
75–115g (3–4oz) blue cheese, such as Roquefort, Fourme d'Ambert or Bleu d'Auvergne

Dressing
1 teaspoon red wine vinegar
1 tablespoon wholegrain or Dijon mustard
salt and freshly ground black pepper
2½ tablespoons grapeseed oil
1½ tablespoons walnut oil

1. Separate the leaves and put into a salad bowl. Sprinkle over the nuts and crumble or chop the cheese over the leaves.

2. Whisk together the vinegar, mustard and seasoning, then slowly pour in the oils, whisking.

3. Just before serving, pour the dressing over the salad and toss lightly.

VARIATION

Creamy Blue Cheese Dressing (for more delicate leaves)

1. Crush 40g (1½oz) blue cheese in a bowl, then whisk in 1 tablespoon white wine vinegar and 5 tablespoons whipping cream.

2. Add 1 tablespoon chopped chives, and black pepper (salt may not be necessary, depending on the saltiness of the cheese).

3. Serve with round or cos lettuce leaves, or corn salad (*mâchée*).

· MUSHROOM SALAD WITH ANCHOVY DRESSING ·

THIS is a robust salad, best accompanied by bread with flavour, such as medium or light rye, Granary, wholemeal or walnut (providing it is not sweet). If serving this salad as a first course, choose a main dish that will not fade into insignificance after it, such as Baked Chicken with Rosemary (see page 72), Pork with Basil and Garlic Stuffing (see page 63), or Sausages Braised with Lentils (see page 70).

SERVES 4

12 anchovy fillets
1 clove garlic
1 tablespoon white wine vinegar or
    tarragon vinegar
3 tablespoons olive oil
freshly ground black pepper

150g (5oz) chestnut (brown)
    mushrooms, chopped
1 small head curly endive
4 sticks celery, sliced
55g (2oz) walnuts, chopped

1. Pound four anchovy fillets with the garlic, then mix in the vinegar. Very slowly add the oil, mixing constantly. Season with black pepper.

2. Toss the mushrooms with the endive and celery, then divide between four plates. Cross two anchovy fillets on top of each serving. Pour the dressing over the salads, sprinkle with the chopped nuts, and serve.

· GREEN SALAD ·

A GOOD green salad will happily partner all sorts of main and light meals, and snacks, or act as a palate cleanser after a rich main course. It can be served either before or with the cheese, and can even be the first course of an otherwise lengthy, rich or heavy meal. Here I give a choice of two dressings.

SERVES 4

4 crisp hearts of cos lettuce, broken into leaves
10 walnut kernels, as fresh as possible, halved
1 tablespoon chervil leaves

Dressing 1
4 tablespoons olive oil
1 tablespoon walnut oil
2 tablespoons white wine vinegar

2 tablespoons crème fraîche or double cream
salt and freshly ground black pepper

Dressing 2
100ml (4fl oz) whipping cream
juice of 2 lemons
1 shallot, very finely chopped
salt and freshly ground black pepper

1. First make your chosen dressing. To make **Dressing 1**, whisk together the oils and vinegar, then very slowly whisk in the cream. Season to taste. To make **Dressing 2**, mix together the cream and lemon juice, then stir in the chopped shallot and seasoning.

2. Pour the chosen dressing over the lettuce hearts, then scatter over the nuts, followed by the chervil.

CHAPTER TWO

FISH & SHELLFISH

FISH AND SHELLFISH are ideal for the cook in a hurry, as they cook quickly and can easily be made into interesting dishes. A word of warning though: fish can also easily be overcooked.

Support a good fishmonger, if you can find one, and buy fresh rather than frozen fish. Don't assume that the fresh fish on display has never been frozen – check to see if there is a notice stating that the fish has been thawed.

Fish, especially flat fish such as sole and plaice, rapidly deteriorate after cutting or filleting. So, rather than buying ready-cut pieces or fillets, buy whole fish or pieces cut for you. Ask the fishmonger, or assistant at the wet fish counter, to clean and scale the fish and to carry out any other necessary preparation, such as filleting; don't forget to ask for the skin, trimmings and bones for stock.

Fresh and thawed frozen fish should be kept cool and eaten as soon as possible; certainly on the day of purchase.

Although fish should always be kept chilled, I return it to room temperature about 30 minutes before cooking; if you use chilled fish you will have to increase the cooking time slightly.

· Aïoli Gratinéed Fish ·

AïOLI (garlic mayonnaise) or ordinary mayonnaise, breadcrumbs, cheese, parsley and lemon make an unusually good, tasty and crisp topping for white fish.

SERVES 4

---

1 lemon
4 firm white fish filllets, such as hake, cod or haddock, each weighing about 175–200g (6–7oz)
4 tablespoons aïoli (see below) or mayonnaise
4 tablespoons fresh breadcrumbs

6 tablespoons grated mature Cantal or Cheddar cheese
1½ tablespoons chopped parsley
a pinch of cayenne pepper
salt and freshly ground black pepper
about 55g (2oz) unsalted butter

---

1. Preheat the grill and line the grill pan with foil. Grate the rind from ½ the lemon. Lay the fillets in the grill pan, squeeze over the lemon juice, then spread with aioli or mayonnaise.

2. Mix together the breadcrumbs, cheese, parsley, lemon rind, cayenne pepper and seasoning. Divide the mixture between the fish fillets, pressing it on lightly, and dot with butter.

3. Cook as far away from the grill as possible for 10–15 minutes (depending on the thickness of the fish), until the topping is crisp and golden and the fish just cooked through. Carefully transfer the fish to warm plates, using a fish slice.

Aïoli

To make aioli, put 2–3 plump cloves garlic and a pinch of salt in a blender and mix together. Blend in a size 1 egg yolk. Then, with the motor running, very slowly pour in 175 ml (6fl oz) olive oil, as when making mayonnaise. Add 1–1½ tablespoons lemon juice, and seasoning to taste.

VARIATION

Instead of the aïoli topping, you can flavour 4 tablespoons soft cheese with chopped herbs and crushed garlic, mix with an equal quantity of fresh breadcrumbs, then spread over fish fillets before grilling.

· MONKFISH WITH GRILLED RED PEPPER SAUCE ·

GRILLING the red peppers gives them a seductive smoky taste as well as softening the skin, but you can miss this stage out. If you do, I suggest making the dressing with 2 tablespoons each olive oil and hazelnut or walnut oil. If you don't remove the skin from the monkfish, you'll find that the fish curls when it cooks, due to the skin shrinking.

SERVES 4
---

2 red peppers
1 small clove garlic, skin on
675g (1½lb) monkfish tail
salt and freshly ground black
   pepper

4 tablespoons olive oil, plus extra
   for brushing
1 tablespoon sherry vinegar

---

1. Preheat the grill. Cut the peppers in half lengthways and grill, skin-side up, with the garlic, until the skin is evenly charred and blackened. Leave until cool enough to handle.

2. Meanwhile, remove the fine membrane from the monkfish, and cut out the backbone to leave two long fillets. Cut across the fillets to make four portions. Season these and brush with oil.

3. Grill the monkfish fillets for about 5 minutes on each side.

4. Meanwhile, skin, core, seed and roughly chop the red peppers. Peel the garlic and put into a blender with the peppers, vinegar, oil and seasoning. Mix together, then pour into a small saucepan and warm gently without allowing the sauce to boil, whisking frequently.

5. Serve the monkfish with some of the red pepper sauce poured over and accompanied by the remainder.

· GRILLED COD WITH CAPER AND ANCHOVY BUTTER ·

THE COMBINATION of sharp and salty capers and anchovies beaten into butter lifts plain grilled cod into something altogether more special.

SERVES 4

4 fillets of cod, each weighing about 175g (6oz)
salt and freshly ground black pepper
olive oil
115g (4oz) unsalted butter, at room temperature

1 tablespoon capers
1 tablespoon anchovy paste
juice of ½ lemon
4 lemon wedges

1. Preheat the grill. Season the cod, brush with olive oil, then grill for 3–4 minutes on each side.

2. Meanwhile, beat the butter to soften it. Chop the capers, then beat them into the butter with the anchovy paste. Add lemon juice and black pepper to taste.

3. Divide the anchovy and caper butter between the four fish fillets and serve straight away with lemon wedges.

VARIATION

Cod with Caper and Lemon Butter

Beat the grated rind and juice of ½ lemon, 3 tablespoons finely chopped parsley and 2 tablespoons finely chopped capers into the softened butter.

· FRESH COD WITH TOMATO VINAIGRETTE ·

I PREFER to prepare the vinaigrette before cooking the fish to give the individual flavours time to blend together, but if you are in a real hurry you can prepare it while the fish is cooking.

SERVES 2

2 spring onions
1 small clove garlic
2 tablespoons white wine vinegar
1½ teaspoons Dijon mustard
100ml (3½fl oz) virgin olive oil, plus extra for brushing
300g (10oz) well-flavoured tomatoes, peeled if liked (see below), seeded and chopped

2 tablespoons chopped chives
1 tablespoon chopped tarragon
salt and freshly ground black pepper
2 fresh cod, salmon or trout fillets

1. Preheat the grill. Finely chop the spring onions and garlic together, then mix with the vinegar and mustard. Slowly pour in the oil, whisking constantly. Add the tomatoes, herbs and seasoning.

2. Brush the fish with olive oil and season with black pepper. Grill the fillets for 3–4 minutes on each side, brushing with oil when they are turned. Cook until the fish is browned and the flesh flakes when tested with the point of a knife.

3. Transfer the fish to warm plates, spoon some of the vinaigrette on top and serve the rest separately.

To Peel and Seed Tomatoes

To peel tomatoes, nick the skin with the point of a sharp knife, then immerse the tomatoes in boiling water for 8–15 seconds, depending on ripeness. Remove from the water and leave until cool enough to handle. Peel off the skin.

To seed tomatoes, cut across into halves and scrape out the seeds and juice.

· HADDOCK WITH FRESH TOMATO SAUCE & CHIVES ·

COD can be substituted for haddock as a companion to this lightly cooked, full-flavoured tomato sauce topped with chive oil.

SERVES 2

100ml (3½fl oz) olive oil
1 shallot
1½ cloves garlic
1 anchovy fillet, chopped
225g (½lb) well-flavoured tomatoes,
  peeled if liked (see page 44)
1–2 teaspoons sun-dried tomato
  paste or tomato purée

about 400g (14oz) haddock fillet,
  skin on, halved
½ bunch of chives
a squeeze of lemon juice
salt and freshly ground black
  pepper

---

1. Heat half the oil in a medium saucepan. Meanwhile, finely chop the shallot and 1 clove of garlic together. Add to the oil with the anchovy, stirring to break up the anchovy. Cook gently for 3–4 minutes.

2. Seed and chop the tomatoes, then add them to the pan with the tomato paste or purée and cook gently until softened.

3. Heat 1 tablespoon oil in a non-stick frying pan. Add the fish, skin-side down, and cook for 3 minutes until the skin is starting to crisp. Turn the fish over and cook for a further 2 minutes.

4. Meanwhile, mix the remaining garlic and oil, the chives, lemon juice, and seasoning to taste, in a blender.

5. Season the tomatoes, adding little if any salt because of the saltiness of the anchovies but plenty of black pepper.

6. Divide the tomato sauce between two warm plates, place the pieces of fish on top, trickle the chive oil over the fish, and serve.

· SKATE WITH BROWN BUTTER ·

Don't be put off by skate that smells of ammonia – this is perfectly normal and the smell will disappear when the fish is cooked.

SERVES 2

2 tablespoons olive oil
2 small–medium skate wings, each
    weighing about 225g (½lb)
several sprigs of parsley
55g (2oz) unsalted butter, diced
2 teaspoons red or white wine
    vinegar

1½ teaspoons capers
salt and freshly ground black
    pepper
2 lemon wedges

1. Heat the oil in a large frying pan over a high heat, add the skate and cook for about 4 minutes on each side (depending on the thickness), until the flesh comes off the bone.

2. Meanwhile, finely chop the parsley.

3. Drain the fish on paper towels, then transfer to warm plates. Sprinkle over the parsley, cover and keep warm.

4. Wipe out the pan with paper towels, and return it to the stove. Heat the butter until it turns a nutty brown. Immediately remove the pan from the stove, add the vinegar, capers and seasoning, then pour over the fish. Serve with lemon wedges.

· SOLE WITH MUSHROOMS ·

DOVER sole is far more expensive than lemon sole, but its texture and flavour are correspondingly superior and combine better with the mushrooms. If I don't feel like spending the money on Dover sole, I prefer to use brill rather than lemon sole for this dish.

SERVES 4

55g (2oz) unsalted butter, diced
1–2 cloves garlic, finely chopped
10 oyster mushrooms, sliced
1 lemon, halved
4 tablespoons medium-bodied dry
   white wine

4 double fillets of Dover sole, or 4
   brill fillets, each weighing about
   175g (6oz)
salt and freshly ground black
   pepper
sprigs of basil, tarragon or parsley

1. Melt half the butter in a large frying pan, add the garlic and mushrooms, and squeeze over some lemon juice. Cook gently for about 5 minutes, stirring occasionally, until softened.

2. Add the wine to the pan and allow to bubble for about 2 minutes.

3. Lower the heat and lay the fish on top of the mushrooms. Squeeze some lemon juice over the fillets and baste with the cooking juices. Cook for 3 minutes, then turn over the fish, baste again and cook for a further 2 minutes.

4. Season the fish and transfer to warm plates. Stir the remaining butter and seasoning into the mushrooms, then spoon over and around the fish. Garnish with sprigs of basil, tarragon or parsley, and serve.

· QUICK SOLE MEUNIÈRE ·

IN THE classic version of *Sole Meunière*, clarified butter is used and the pan is wiped clean after frying the fish; then more butter is added, heated until it browns, and poured over the fish with lemon juice. For my quick variation, I use ordinary butter and simply add lemon juice to the pan immediately after cooking the fish.

Delicate fish, like sole, cooks and tastes best when left on the bone but if you are really pushed for time you could use fillets rather than whole fish. Allow 3–4 minutes a side, and bear in mind that lemon sole takes less time than Dover.

——————————— SERVES 2 ———————————

2 small Dover or lemon sole
seasoned plain flour
40g (1½oz) unsalted butter
juice of ½ lemon

1 tablespoon chopped parsley
salt and freshly ground black
    pepper

1. Coat the fish lightly in seasoned flour.

2. Heat the butter in a large frying pan until fairly hot but do not allow it to colour. Add the fish and cook for about 5 minutes on each side.

3. Transfer the fish to warmed plates, cover and keep warm. Squeeze the lemon juice into the pan, add the parsley and seasoning, then pour over the fish. Serve immediately.

· HALIBUT WITH COURGETTES AND BASIL ·

THE fish (I have used halibut, but monkfish escalopes or plaice, sole or brill fillets can also be used) is braised on a bed of courgettes spiked with garlic and basil so it remains moist and is well-flavoured. The braising bed is then puréed to make a light sauce.

SERVES 4

65g (2½oz) unsalted butter, diced
1 clove garlic, crushed
300g (10oz) small courgettes, diced
10 basil leaves
2 tablespoons fish stock or medium-bodied dry white wine
4 halibut escalopes, each weighing about 150–175g (5–6oz)

1 well-flavoured tomato, seeded (see page 44) and chopped (optional)
salt and freshly ground black pepper
lemon juice

---

1. Heat 25g (1oz) butter in a large frying pan, add the garlic and courgettes and cook for about 2 minutes.

2. Stir in the basil and stock or wine, then lay the fish on top. Scatter the tomato, if using, over the fish. Season, bring to the boil, cover and cook gently for about 10 minutes until the fish is cooked through.

3. Transfer the fish to a warmed dish, cover and keep warm. If the courgettes are not tender, continue to simmer until they are.

4. Mix the courgettes and remaining butter in a blender or food processor until fairly smooth. Add 1–2 tablespoons hot fish stock or water, if necessary, to make a soft purée. Return to the pan, add lemon juice to taste, and heat through.

5. Serve the sauce with the fish.

· FISH PARCELS WITH HERBS ·

A SIMPLE, light, trouble-free recipe. The parcels can also be baked in an oven preheated to 200°C/400°F/Gas Mark 6, in which case I prefer to use greaseproof paper instead of foil.

SERVES 4

4 red mullet, sea bream or trout, each weighing about 225–300g (8–10oz), cleaned and scaled
2 tablespoons mixed herbs such as parsley, basil, thyme, tarragon and fennel

1 clove garlic, finely chopped
2 tablespoons lemon juice
3 tablespoons virgin or extra virgin olive oil
salt and freshly ground black pepper

1. Cut four large pieces of foil and place a fish in the centre of each piece.

2. Bring a steamer containing a few inches of water to the boil.

3. Meanwhile, mix together the herbs, garlic and lemon juice, then slowly pour in the oil, whisking constantly with a fork or a small balloon whisk. Season to taste, then spoon some of the herb mixture inside each fish and pour the remainder over the top. Fold the foil over each fish and twist the edges together to seal tightly.

4. Put the parcels in a steaming basket, cover and put on the steamer base. Steam for about 15 minutes, depending on the thickness of the fish.

5. Serve the fish in the unopened parcels.

· BUTTERED BAKED SALMON ·

LIKE poultry and meat, fish is more succulent and tastes better when cooked whole or in a large piece, rather than as fillets or individual portions. But, unlike poultry and meat, it is possible to cook large pieces of fish in a short time – here, just 15 minutes. Seasoned but undressed small spinach leaves make a good accompaniment.

115g (4oz) unsalted butter, diced
1kg (2lb) piece boned middle cut of
  salmon
1 tablespoon dried dill

2 tablespoons wholegrain mustard
a squeeze of lemon juice
salt and freshly ground black
  pepper

1. Preheat the oven to 230°C/450°F/Gas Mark 8. Gently melt the butter in a small saucepan.

2. Meanwhile, open the salmon and press along the backbone so it lies almost flat. Place in a shallow baking dish, skin-side up.

3. Mix the dill, mustard, lemon juice and seasoning into the butter, and pour over the salmon. Bake for about 15 minutes, basting a couple of times, until the flesh just flakes when tested with the point of a knife.

4. Cut the salmon into thick slices and serve with the buttery juices.

· SALMON COOKED ON ONE SIDE ·

SALMON cooked on one side – *saumon à l'unilatéral* – has become very popular in France. As t he fish remains quite rare, it must be very fresh and should not have been frozen, so that it is moist and full of flavour. If you prefer salmon better-cooked, cover the pan and cook for a further 2–3 minutes.

4 salmon fillets, skin on, each
  weighing about 150g (5oz)
olive oil

40g (1½oz) unsalted butter, diced
sea salt

1. Brush the salmon skin with oil. Heat the butter in a large frying pan over a moderate heat. Cook the salmon, skin-side down, until the skin is brown and crisp and the flesh has just begun to change colour.

2. Transfer to warmed plates, sprinkle lightly with sea salt and serve straight away.

· SALMON WITH PARSLEY, LEMON AND DILL ·

SALMON is no longer the rare and expensive treat it used to be. Even so, it always seems special, so this very simple, everyday recipe could easily be served when entertaining. The egg, flour and herb mixture makes a crisp coating that keeps the salmon succulent and gives an interesting contrast in texture.

———————————— SERVES 4 ————————————

1 large lemon
4 pieces skinned salmon fillet, each
   weighing about 150g (5oz)
2 teaspoons plain flour
1½ tablespoons chopped parsley

1½ tablespoons chopped dill
salt and freshly ground black
   pepper
2 small eggs, lightly beaten
2–3 tablespoons olive oil

1. Cut the lemon in half and squeeze the juice of one half over the salmon.

2. Mix together the flour, herbs and seasoning, then slowly stir in the eggs, keeping the mixture smooth.

3. Heat the oil in a frying pan. Dip each piece of fish in the egg and herb mixture so it is completely coated. Then cook in the oil for about 3 minutes on each side, until cooked through and a light golden colour.

4. Transfer the fish to paper towels to drain. Cut the remaining half lemon into four wedges and serve with the salmon.

· Salmon with Bacon and Horseradish ·

THIS recipe originates in Alsace and I highly recommend serving it with 125g (4oz) green lentils cooked with a clove-studded ½ onion, a small clove of garlic and a bouquet garni. Just cover the lentils with water and cook until most of the liquid has been absorbed and the lentils are soupy. Discard the onion, garlic and bouquet garni and season to taste.

SERVES 2

2 salmon steaks, each weighing
   about 175g (6oz)
55g (2oz) lardons or diced thick-cut
   streaky bacon
20g (¾oz) unsalted butter
salt and freshly ground black
   pepper

1 large shallot
150ml (5fl oz) crème fraîche
1 tablespoon grated horseradish or
   1½–2 tablespoons bottled
   horseradish

1. Preheat the grill. Using the point of a knife, make holes in both sides of each piece of salmon, then insert a piece of bacon in each hole. Rub the salmon with butter, place in a shallow flameproof dish and cook about 9cm (3½ inches) from the grill for 3–4 minutes on each side. Transfer the salmon to a warmed plate, season, cover and keep warm.

2. Meanwhile, finely chop the shallot.

3. Pour the fat from the dish, then stir the crème fraîche into the dish to dissolve the cooking juices. Add the horseradish, shallot and seasoning and simmer for 2 minutes if serving with the lentils (slightly longer if not) until lightly thickened. Serve with the salmon, and lentils if using.

· SALMON WITH RED WINE ·

DESPITE the common maxim 'white wine goes with fish', red wine can sometimes partner fish, particularly salmon, very satisfactorily. The wine does need to be chosen with some care – a heavy, tannic or acidic one would be a disaster. However, a soft, fruity wine, such as Chinon, works admirably.

SERVES 2

25g (1oz) unsalted butter, diced
2 salmon cutlets, each weighing
  about 175g (6oz)
150ml (5fl oz) soft, fruity red wine
  such as Chinon

1 tablespoon chopped tarragon
salt and freshly ground black
  pepper
tarragon leaves

1. Heat half the butter in a non-stick frying pan, add the salmon and cook each side briefly over a high heat. Lower the heat and cook for about 3 minutes on each side until the flesh just flakes when tested with the point of a sharp knife.

2. Transfer the fish to a warmed plate, cover and keep warm.

3. Stir the wine into the pan, then boil until reduced by half. Add the tarragon and seasoning. Remove the pan from the heat and gradually add the remaining butter, a piece at a time, stirring vigorously.

4. Divide the sauce between two warmed plates, place the salmon on top and garnish with tarragon leaves.

· SCALLOPS WITH PARSLEY AND WHITE WINE ·

I LOVE fresh, sweet scallops, especially when cooked in a sympathetic, light, clean-tasting way such as this. Ask the fishmonger to shell the scallops for you, as he should be able to do it in a fraction of the time.

SERVES 4 AS A FIRST COURSE;
2 AS A MAIN COURSE

25g (1oz) unsalted butter
1 tablespoon olive oil
1 shallot, finely chopped
1 clove garlic, crushed
about 16 scallops, depending on
  size, shelled

115ml (4fl oz) medium-bodied dry
  white wine
juice of 1 lemon
2½–3 tablespoons chopped parsley
salt and freshly ground black
  pepper

1. Heat the butter and oil in a frying pan, add the shallot and garlic and cook until softened but not coloured.

2. Meanwhile, remove the orange corals from the scallops, and reserve. Then cut the scallops horizontally into two or three slices, depending on size.

3. Pour the wine into the pan and allow to boil until reduced by about half. Add the scallops, and about 30 seconds later the corals, and cook briefly until just turning opaque. Squeeze over the lemon juice and quickly add the parsley and seasoning.

4. Serve the scallops straight away, with the juices spooned over.

· GRILLED PRAWNS WITH WARM HERB BUTTER ·

THIS dish requires the minimum of effort and attention, leaving you plenty of time to spend on the rest of the meal, or allowing you to prepare an extremely quick meal if followed by a simple main course such as Chicken with Herbs (see page 71).

Eat the prawns with your fingers, peeling off the shells and dipping the prawns in the herb butter. Don't forget to provide napkins or finger bowls.

SERVES 4 AS A FIRST COURSE

about 55g (2oz) unsalted butter
about 675g (1½lb) raw king
   prawns, shells on

a handful of herbs such as dill,
   tarragon, basil, parsley and
   chives
juice of ½ lemon

1. Preheat the grill and put a saucepan of water on to heat. Dice the butter, put it in a small bowl and place over the saucepan to melt.

2. Grill the prawns for 1½–2 minutes on each side until they are sizzling and pink.

3. Meanwhile, finely chop the herbs, add them to the butter, and squeeze in the lemon juice. Serve the prawns with the butter for dipping.

· PRAWNS WITH PERNOD ·

As WITH most things in life, when buying prawns you get what you pay for. Although king prawns are more expensive than smaller ones, they do have a much better flavour and texture and I think are the most appropriate for this recipe. However you could use smaller ones if you prefer; if using already cooked ones they will just need to be heated through, which takes about the same time.

Use the prawn shells, heads and legs to make a well-flavoured fish stock.

SERVES 3–4 AS A FIRST COURSE; 2 AS A MAIN COURSE

550g (1¼lb) raw king prawns, shells on
3 tablespoons olive oil
2 cloves garlic, crushed
1–2 tablespoons Pernod or other anise liqueur

2 tablespoons chopped parsley
salt and freshly ground black pepper
plump lemon wedges

1. Peel the prawns and remove the heads and fine legs.

2. Heat the oil in a frying pan, add the garlic and prawns and fry quickly for 2–3 minutes until the prawns turn bright pink.

3. Stir in the liqueur, parsley and seasoning and bring to the boil. Serve the prawns straight away, with the cooking juices spooned over, accompanied by lemon wedges.

· MUSSELS IN A CREAMY HERB SAUCE ·

SERVE with lots of fresh, crusty bread, and perhaps a crisp green salad (see page 39) to follow.

Farmed mussels, which most mussels on sale now are, are cleaner and contain less grit, if any, than wild ones. You can buy cleaned and prepared mussels, although you will have to pay extra for them. If you are not using these, remove the fibrous beards, using a small sharp knife, then rinse the mussels under cold running water.

SERVES 2

25g (1oz) unsalted butter
2 shallots, finely chopped
2 cloves garlic, finely chopped
225ml (8fl oz) medium-bodied dry
   white wine
fresh bouquet garni, including
   parsley, thyme and chives
freshly ground black pepper

1kg (2lb) cleaned mussels
2–4 tablespoons crème fraîche,
   soured cream, or fromage frais
3–4 tablespoons chopped mixed
   herbs such as tarragon, chives,
   parsley and fennel
lemon juice (optional)

1. Swirl the butter in a large saucepan, add the shallots and garlic, and cook for about 2 minutes. Pour in the wine, add the bouquet garni and black pepper and bring to the boil.

2. Tip the mussels into the pan, cover and return to the boil. Boil for about 4 minutes, shaking the pan occasionally, until all the mussels have opened. Discard any that remain closed.

3. Transfer the mussels to warmed large soup plates or bowls, cover and keep warm.

4. Discard the bouquet garni and boil the cooking juices for 1 minute. Then, over a low heat, stir in the crème fraîche, soured cream or fromage frais and the herbs. Add a squeeze of lemon juice if liked, pour over the mussels and serve straight away.

CHAPTER THREE

MEAT & POULTRY

VEGETARIANISM and snack meals have been much slower to catch on in France than in Britain, and meat, poultry or game is still *de rigueur* for the main course, particularly at dinnertime.

Quick cooking needs tender, lean cuts, such as lamb noisettes, chops and steaks, pork noisettes and escalopes, sirloin and rump steaks, or fillet if you can afford it. Thin pieces cook more quickly than thick ones but can become dry, unless cooked in a sauce, as in Pork with Prunes (see page 62).

Efforts are now being made to produce meat and poultry that has more flavour (as well as being more humanely reared). Predictably, we do have to pay more for such meat and poultry, but I'm prepared to cut down on lesser-quality produce for the sake of an occasional treat.

I make sure that meat and poultry are at room temperature when I cook them, not only so they will cook more quickly, but also because they will be more succulent. If you use meat or poultry straight from the refrigerator you will have to increase the cooking time accordingly.

· STEAK WITH HERB SAUCE ·

THIS simple, herby, sharp, clean-tasting green sauce beautifully complements thick, juicy prime-quality beef. The sauce can also be served with pork.

SERVES 4

2 cloves garlic
2 tablespoons capers, preferably
   dry packed in salt
a large bunch of basil
a large bunch of parsley
1 tablespoon Dijon mustard
1 tablespoon wine vinegar

150ml (5fl oz) olive oil, plus extra
   for brushing
salt and freshly ground black
   pepper
4 rump steaks, each weighing about
   175g (6oz), and about 3.25cm
   (1¼ inches) thick

---

1. Preheat the grill. Put the garlic, capers, herbs, mustard and vinegar in a food processor and mix until evenly chopped. With the motor still running, slowly pour in the oil. Season and set aside.

2. Brush the steaks with just enough oil to make them shiny, and season with black pepper. Grill for 3–3½ minutes on each side so the steaks stay rare, succulent and flavourful.

3. Transfer the steaks to warmed plates, sprinkle with salt and serve with the herb sauce.

· STEAK WITH SHALLOT AND RED WINE SAUCE ·

THIS sauce is a classic, and should be made with the same wine that you are going to drink. For an even quicker dish, use minute steaks, which need only 1–2 minutes cooking on each side.

SERVES 2

1 tablespoon olive oil
25g (1oz) unsalted butter, diced
2 sirloin or rump steaks
1 shallot
6–8 sprigs of parsley

115ml (4fl oz) medium-bodied red wine
a sprig of thyme
salt and freshly ground black pepper

1. Heat the oil and half the butter in a frying pan, add the steaks and fry quickly for 2 minutes on each side. Then lower the heat slightly until cooked to your liking.

2. Meanwhile, finely chop the shallot. Strip the leaves from the parsley and chop finely.

3. Transfer the steaks to two warmed plates, cover and keep warm. Stir the shallot into the pan and cook for about 2 minutes. Stir in the wine, add the thyme, and boil to thicken slightly and concentrate the flavour.

4. Discard the thyme. Stir in most of the parsley and the seasoning, remove the pan from the heat and gradually swirl in the remaining butter to thicken the sauce.

5. Pour over the steaks, sprinkle with the remaining parsley, and serve.

· PORK WITH PRUNES ·

At ONE time highly renowned prunes were prepared around Tours in the Loire valley, and they found their way into many local dishes, the most well-known of which is *porc au pruneaux*.

As is so often the case, the local wine, in this case Vouvray, is the most suitable to use in the dish, and to drink with it. Vouvray, one of my favourite white wines, is produced in all styles: still and sparkling; dry, medium and sweet. (A good sweet Vouvray ages beautifully to be almost on a par with the best Sauternes.) This dish requires a dry Vouvray but it will not be bone-dry, like Muscadet.

Pork escalopes cook quickly but they can dry out during cooking. This is prevented in this recipe, firstly by cooking the escalopes gently so they do not toughen, and secondly by cooking them in stock and wine, which they soak up.

SERVES 4

25g (1oz) butter
8 pork escalopes
200ml (7fl oz) dry Vouvray or
 similar fruity dry white wine
12 no-soak prunes

200ml (7fl oz) veal stock
1–2 teaspoons redcurrant jelly
lemon juice (optional)
salt and freshly ground black
 pepper

1. Heat the butter in a wide frying pan, add the pork and cook over a high heat to quickly brown the outside. Remove from the pan.

2. Stir the wine into the pan, add the prunes, then boil hard for 2–3 minutes. Add the stock and bring back to the boil.

3. Return the pork to the pan and cook gently for about 7 minutes until tender, turning once.

4. Transfer the pork to a warmed dish, cover and keep warm.

5. Boil the cooking juices hard until lightly syrupy. Stir in the redcurrant jelly and boil until slightly thickened. Add some lemon juice if liked, and seasoning to taste.

6. Either return the escalopes to the pan and turn them in the sauce for about a minute, so they absorb some of it, and then serve. Or pour the sauce over the pork and serve straight away.

· PORK WITH BASIL AND GARLIC STUFFING ·

THIS light stuffing of chopped fragrant basil and garlic imbues the pork with a seductive flavour. Lean and tender pork tenderloins usually weigh about 350g (12oz), and cook quickly. Cooked meat cuts better if allowed to 'rest' for about 10 minutes after cooking. So, if possible, try to schedule the meal so the pork is cooked before you eat the first course.

SERVES 2

6 cloves garlic
350g (12oz) pork tenderloin
3 tablespoons chopped basil
finely grated rind and juice of
   1 lemon

salt and freshly ground black
   pepper
2 tablespoons olive oil
1 large fresh bay leaf, chopped
lemon slices

1. Add the garlic to a small saucepan of boiling water, and return to the boil for 1 minute. Drain and rinse under cold water. Cut any large cloves in half.

2. Using a sharp knife, slit the pork lengthways without cutting right the way through. Open the pork out and sprinkle the inside evenly with basil and lemon rind. Lay the garlic evenly along the middle of the pork, on top of the basil and lemon. Season. Close the pork and tie securely at 2.5cm (1 inch) intervals with string. Cut the tenderloin across to make two pieces.

3. Heat the oil in a flameproof casserole that the pork just fits. Add the pork and quickly brown evenly. Pour over the lemon juice and add the bay leaf. Then cook over a moderate heat, turning the pork occasionally and basting frequently, for about 10–15 minutes or until the pork is cooked through.

4. If time allows, cover the pork and leave in a warm place while you eat the first course. Cut the pork into slices and serve with the lemon slices.

· LAMB WITH FLAGEOLET BEANS ·

ALONG with other types of dried beans, pale green flageolet beans are one of the few products that are not adversely affected by canning, so I always have a can handy in the cupboard. Their flavour combines well with lamb, and they purée easily to make a quick sauce.

———————————— SERVES 2 ————————————

3 cloves garlic
1 small onion
1 × 400g (14oz) can flageolet
  beans
salt and freshly ground black
  pepper

4 lamb steaks, each weighing about
  150g (5oz)
1–2 tablespoons virgin olive oil,
  plus extra for brushing
a small handful of parsley sprigs

1. Preheat the grill. Put two cloves of garlic in a saucepan, cover with cold water and simmer, while you chop the onion and drain the beans. Add both to the pan, with sufficient water to just cover the beans. Season and heat through for about 5 minutes.

2. Meanwhile, crush the remaining garlic clove and rub over the lamb. Brush with oil, season with pepper, then grill for about 4 minutes on each side.

3. Meanwhile, coarsely chop about 3 tablespoons parsley.

4. If liked, scoop out about a quarter of the beans and keep warm in a dish over a bowl of hot water, if liked. Purée the remaining beans with the parsley and oil; add more water if necessary to make a fairly thick sauce. Reheat briefly.

5. Serve the lamb steaks on the sauce, accompanied by the whole beans if reserved.

Opposite: Duck with Peaches (page 83) served with Quick Potato Gratin (page 86)

· LAMB WITH MINT SAUCE AND GRILLED TOMATOES ·

No, I have not included a recipe from this side of the Channel – this is a very different mint sauce. I came across it in a simple restaurant near Valence about four years ago. I ordered the dish out of curiosity (all the French people I know who have tried English mint sauce with lamb are far from complimentary about it). What arrived was a fragrant, green, coarse paste that beautifully complemented the sweet lamb, the whole affect rounded off by flavourful, lightly grilled tomatoes.

SERVES 4

1 large clove garlic
leaves from a small bunch of mint
40g (1½oz) walnuts
salt and freshly ground black
  pepper
5 tablespoons olive oil, plus extra
  for brushing
8 loin lamb chops, each weighing
  about 115g (4oz) and about

2.5cm (1 inch) thick

Tomatoes
4 well-flavoured tomatoes, halved
4 teaspoons olive oil
4–6 tablespoons freshly grated
  Parmesan
freshly ground black pepper

1. Preheat the grill. Put the garlic, mint, walnuts and salt and pepper in a small blender; mix briefly. Then, with the motor running, slowly pour in the oil until the mixture forms a thick paste. Transfer to a bowl.

2. Season the lamb chops, and brush with oil. Grill for 4 minutes on each side so that the lamb is still pink in the centre.

3. Meanwhile, sprinkle the cut surfaces of the tomatoes with the oil, Parmesan and pepper and add to the grill rack when turning the lamb.

4. Spoon some of the mint sauce on to each chop and serve, accompanied by the tomatoes.

Opposite: Baked Chicken with Rosemary (page 72) served with Crumbed Broccoli (page 96) and Jacket Onions (page 87)

· LAMB WITH MUSHROOMS AND TOMATOES ·

THIS is a simple sauté, the lamb being cooked quickly at a high temperature while you shake the pan to keep the meat on the move.

SERVES 2

15g (½oz) unsalted butter
1 tablespoon olive oil
300–350g (10–12oz) lean lamb,
   cut into 7.5 × 2.5cm (3 × 1 inch)
   strips
1 clove garlic
3 spring onions, white part only
115g (4oz) chestnut (brown)
   mushrooms

2 well-flavoured tomatoes
5 tablespoons medium-bodied dry
   white wine
2 tablespoons vegetable or veal
   stock, or water
salt and freshly ground black
   pepper
chopped thyme, tarragon or parsley

1. Heat the butter and oil in a frying pan over a fairly high heat, add the lamb and cook for about 2½ minutes on each side.

2. Meanwhile, finely chop the garlic and spring onions, slice the mushrooms, and seed and chop the tomatoes.

3. Transfer the lamb to a warmed plate, cover and keep warm.

4. Stir the garlic, spring onions and mushrooms into the pan and cook for about 2 minutes. Add the tomatoes, wine, stock or water, and seasoning, and bubble for another minute or so.

5. Return the meat to the pan, baste with the vegetables and heat together for about 2 minutes. Serve sprinkled with thyme, tarragon or parsley.

· LAMB WITH MUSTARD DRESSING, GARLIC ·
AND COURGETTES

THE flavour of the garlic is softened by boiling for 5 minutes, then grilling the cloves whole. When the dish is served, squeeze the garlic cloves from their skins, mash with the dressing and eat the resulting purée with the lamb.

SERVES 2

6 large cloves garlic, unpeeled
2 tablespoons lemon juice
2 tablespoons wholegrain mustard
4 tablespoons olive oil, plus extra
 for brushing
1 tablespoon chopped thyme

salt and freshly ground black
 pepper
4 loin lamb chops, each weighing
 about 115g (4oz) and about
 2.5cm (1 inch) thick
225g (½lb) small courgettes

1. Boil the garlic cloves for 5 minutes.

2. Meanwhile, preheat the grill. Whisk the lemon juice into the mustard, then slowly pour in the oil, whisking constantly. Add the thyme and seasoning, then brush the lamb chops liberally with the dressing and put on the grill rack.

3. Slice the courgettes lengthways and lay on the grill rack.

4. Drain the garlic and add to the grill rack. Brush the vegetables with oil and sprinkle with seasoning. Place the loaded grill pan under the grill for about 8 minutes, turning the lamb halfway through and brushing liberally with the remaining dressing, until the outside is lightly charred and the inside pink.

5. Turn the vegetables halfway through, brushing them with oil; the garlic will be blackened at the end of cooking, but the inside will be tender and juicy.

6. Spoon any remaining dressing, including any juices in the grill pan, over the lamb and serve with the vegetables.

· LAMB NOISETTES WITH A CRISP HERB COATING ·

THE egg makes a barrier between the meat and the breadcrumb coating, keeping the former moist and the latter contrastingly crisp.

If fresh rosemary is not available, you can substitute 1½–2 tablespoons of another herb, such as parsley, thyme or tarragon, or a mixture, which could include chives and basil. Lamb chops or steaks can be used instead of noisettes, but they will take longer to cook – about 5–7 minutes each side.

SERVES 4

40g (1½oz) unsalted butter
2 tablespoons olive oil
75g (3oz) fresh breadcrumbs
1 tablespoon finely chopped
   rosemary
salt and freshly ground black
   pepper

8 lamb noisettes, each weighing
   about 65g (2½oz)
½ egg, beaten
juice of ½ lemon

---

1. Gently melt 25g (1oz) butter and 1 tablespoon oil in a small saucepan, then mix with the breadcrumbs, rosemary and seasoning.

2. Dip the noisettes in the egg to coat very lightly, then cover liberally with the breadcrumb mixture, pressing it on.

3. Heat the remaining oil in a large, preferably non-stick, frying pan. Add the noisettes and cook for about 3½–5 minutes on each side, turning them carefully to avoid dislodging the coating.

4. Transfer the lamb to a warmed plate, cover and keep warm. Stir the lemon juice into the pan, dislodging the sediment. Bring to the boil, then remove from the heat and stir in the remaining butter. Pour over the lamb and serve.

· LAMB WITH GARLIC SAUCE ·

DON'T be put off by the number of garlic cloves – successive boilings tames their flavour. They are then cooked with milk and bread to make a creamy sauce that won't leave you with the taste of garlic in your mouth for ages afterwards. An even quicker, and richer, version can be made by briefly simmering the blanched garlic in 200ml (7fl oz) cream instead of the milk and bread.

SERVES 4

12 cloves garlic, unpeeled
4 lamb steaks, each weighing
   about 175g (6oz)
olive oil

salt and freshly ground black
   pepper
200ml (7fl oz) milk
1 slice country bread
1 tablespoon chopped parsley

1. Preheat the grill. Put the garlic in a small saucepan of boiling water, boil for 1 minute and drain; repeat twice, using fresh water each time. Squeeze the garlic cloves to pop them out of their skins.

2. Brush the lamb with oil and season with pepper. Cook under a fairly hot grill for about 6 minutes on each side, so the outside is lightly charred and the inside still pink.

3. Meanwhile, gently heat the milk. Tear the bread into pieces and add to the milk, with the garlic. Simmer, stirring occasionally, until thickened to a light sauce, then purée in a food processor or blender.

4. Return the sauce to the pan, add the parsley and seasoning, and reheat. Serve with the lamb.

· Sausages Braised with Lentils ·

SURPRISE everyone by serving a hearty but not heavy meal that seems as if it has taken ages to cook, in less than 30 minutes. Chopped chestnut (brown) mushrooms and/or chopped celery can be included, while sliced leeks could replace two of the shallots. 'Fresh' green and brown lentils will be cooked in 15–20 minutes, but ones that have been in the cupboard for a while will take longer.

SERVES 4

1 tablespoon olive oil
450g (1lb) chunky pork sausages, skinned and cut into large pieces
3 shallots, chopped
1 carrot, chopped
3–4 cloves garlic, crushed
300g (10oz) green or brown lentils

about 625ml (1¼ pints) veal or vegetable stock, or water
1 bay leaf
3–4 sprigs of thyme
several sprigs of parsley
2 well-flavoured tomatoes
salt and freshly ground black pepper

1. Heat the oil in a medium, preferably non-stick, saucepan. Add the sausages, shallots, carrot and garlic and cook until the sausages have browned and the shallots and garlic softened.

2. Stir the lentils into the pan for about 1 minute, then add the stock or water and the herbs. Bring to the boil, cover and simmer for 15–20 minutes or until the lentils are tender and most of the liquid absorbed; keep an eye on the level of stock, or water, and add more if necessary.

3. Meanwhile, seed and chop the tomatoes (see page 44), then add to the lentils with the seasoning. Heat briefly, and serve.

· CHICKEN WITH HERBS ·

THIS is a very simple but nevertheless succulent and well-flavoured dish. If you have time, leave the chicken to marinate for 1–1½ hours before cooking and it will taste even better.

SERVES 4

4 chicken breasts, boned
6 tablespoons olive oil
3 tablespoons lemon juice

leaves from several sprigs of
 marjoram, thyme, tarragon and
 fennel, chopped
salt and freshly ground black
 pepper

1. Put the chicken breasts in a shallow dish, pour over the oil and lemon juice and sprinkle with the herbs and plenty of black pepper. Leave for at least 5–10 minutes.

2. Preheat the grill.

3. Grill the chicken for about 15 minutes, basting frequently with the herb mixture and turning occasionally, until the skin is golden and the flesh cooked through.

· BAKED CHICKEN WITH ROSEMARY ·

BAKING chicken quarters with rosemary, garlic and sun-dried tomatoes gives them plenty of flavour for the minimum of effort. When I'm going to cook this dish, the first thing I do when I get home is to combine the chicken and flavouring ingredients so they have as long as possible to marinate together, thus improving the taste of the dish.

While the oven is heating I prepare the rest of the meal, which usually includes at least one other dish that needs to go in the oven, such as Baked Cinnamon Oranges (see page 103) or Baked Apricots en Papillote with Vanilla (see page 102), and perhaps a first course or vegetable dish that requires some attention, for example Deep-fried Camembert (see page 27) or Asparagus with Quick Hollandaise Sauce (see page 28).

SERVES 2

leaves from a sprig of rosemary, chopped
2 cloves garlic, finely chopped
1½ tablespoons chopped sun-dried tomatoes in oil
2 chicken quarters

salt and freshly ground black pepper
5 tablespoons olive oil, or, preferably, a mixture of olive oil and oil from the sun-dried tomatoes
1½ tablespoons lemon juice

---

1. Sprinkle half the rosemary, garlic and sun-dried tomatoes over the base of a shallow baking dish. Place the chicken portions, skin-side up, on top, and sprinkle with the remaining rosemary, garlic and tomatoes. Season, then pour over the oil and lemon juice and leave to marinate for up to 2 hours.

2. Preheat the oven to 190°C/375°F/Gas Mark 5.

3. Bake the chicken for about 25 minutes, basting the pieces occasionally with the cooking juices, and turning them halfway through.

> **Sun-dried Tomatoes**
> Sun-dried tomatoes are available in dried form, or preserved in oil. The dried ones are cheaper, but they need to be soaked before use. To do this, put into a bowl and cover with hot water. Leave for 1–1½ hours, then remove and dry on paper towels. Put the tomatoes in a jar and cover with olive oil. Use as required. The oil itself will become tomato flavoured and can be used for salad dressings or brushing or crostini and pizzas.

· QUICK CHICKEN POT ROAST WITH THYME ·

By USING chicken drumsticks or thighs you can make a very passable, speedy version of a traditional pot roast.

SERVES 2

1 tablespoon olive oil
25g (1oz) unsalted butter, diced
1 clove garlic, crushed
4 chicken drumsticks or thighs
2 good sprigs of thyme

5 tablespoons medium-bodied dry
   white wine
salt and freshly ground black
   pepper

1. Heat the oil and butter in a heavy, flameproof casserole. Add the garlic and chicken, and brown on one side; then add the thyme, turn the chicken, and brown on the other side.

2. Add the wine, allow to bubble hard for 2–3 minutes, then lower the heat so the wine just bubbles occasionally. Put the lid on the casserole and cook, turning the chicken two or three times, for about 15 minutes or until tender.

3. Transfer the chicken to a warmed serving plate, cover and keep warm. Tilt the casserole, spoon off most of the fat, then return the casserole to a high heat. Stir in 1–2 tablespoons water to dislodge the sediment, season and bring to the boil. Pour over the chicken and serve.

· CHICKEN WITH GRAPES ·

THIS dish always gives the impression of being luxurious and elegant, but there is nothing difficult about the cooking. Courgettes with Almonds (see page 89) and new potatoes are good accompaniments.

SERVES 4

25g (1oz) unsalted butter
1 tablespoon olive oil
1 shallot
1 clove garlic
4 chicken breasts
175ml (6fl oz) fruity white wine, such as a Chenin Blanc

115–150g (4–5oz) seedless green grapes
leaves from 2–3 sprigs of tarragon or thyme
2–3 tablespoons crème fraîche
salt and freshly ground black pepper

1. Heat the butter and oil in a large frying pan. Finely chop the shallot and add to the pan. Cook for 2–3 minutes while crushing the garlic.

2. Slice the chicken breasts in half lengthways, add to the pan and fry for 1½–2 minutes on each side. Stir in the wine, cover the pan and cook gently for about 7–8 minutes, or until the chicken is tender, turning it over halfway through.

3. Meanwhile, halve the grapes and chop just sufficient tarragon or thyme to add a light background flavour.

4. Transfer the chicken to a warmed plate, cover and keep warm.

5. Add the herbs to the cooking juices and boil if necessary to reduce. Stir in the grapes and crème fraîche. Season, heat through, pour the sauce and grapes over the chicken, and serve.

· CHICKEN WITH MUSHROOMS ·

ALTHOUGH this recipe can be enjoyed at any time of the year, it is a particularly good one for the winter when you want something warming and satisfying yet quick to cook.

SERVES 4

1 tablespoon olive oil
15g (½oz) unsalted butter, diced
8 chicken thighs or drumsticks, or a mixture
a large bunch of spring onions
leaves from 3–4 sprigs of tarragon
350g (12oz) chestnut (brown), oyster, shiitake or wild mushrooms, or a mixture

175ml (6fl oz) Vouvray, or similar fruity, medium-dry white wine, or chicken stock
100ml (3½fl oz) crème fraîche
salt and freshly ground black pepper
a few whole tarragon leaves (optional)

1. Heat the oil and butter in a large frying pan, add the chicken and cook over a medium heat until evenly browned.

2. Meanwhile, finely chop the spring onions, chop the tarragon leaves, cut large mushrooms into quarters, and oyster mushrooms into 2.5cm (1 inch) strips. Add all the vegetables and the tarragon to the chicken, cook for 2 minutes, then add the wine or stock. Bring to the boil, partly cover the pan and cook gently, turning the chicken occasionally, for about 15 minutes until the chicken is tender.

3. Using a slotted spoon, transfer the chicken and mushrooms to a warmed dish, cover and keep warm. Boil the cooking liquid until lightly syrupy, then stir in the crème fraîche, season, and boil until slightly thickened.

4. Return the chicken and mushrooms to the pan, turn in the sauce and heat together briefly. Sprinkle over some whole tarragon leaves, if liked, and serve.

· CHICKEN WITH CREAMY MUSTARD & HERB SAUCE ·

THE sauce is self-made, the chicken self-basting, the dish tastes good and there's only a bowl, spoon or fork and a knife to wash up – what more could the cook in a hurry want?

If you are going to use the oven for another dish, such as Herb Custards (see page 14) or Cauliflower and Blue Cheese Parcels (see page 95), you can bake the chicken. Put the parcels on a heated baking sheet and cook on the top shelf of the oven. Increase the temperature to 200°C/400°F/Gas Mark 6, once the other dish has been removed, and cook for a total of about 20 minutes.

SERVES 4

2 tablespoons Dijon mustard
2 tablespoons crème fraîche or
  Greek-style yogurt
about 6 tablespoons chopped
  mixed herbs such as chervil,
  tarragon, dill and parsley

salt and freshly ground black
  pepper
4 skinned chicken breasts, each
  weighing about 150g (5oz)

---

1. Bring a few inches of water to the boil in a steamer or saucepan.

2. Tear four pieces of greaseproof paper, each large enough to hold a chicken breast. Mix together the mustard, crème fraîche or yogurt, herbs and seasoning.

3. Slice the chicken breasts in half lengthways and place two halves on each piece of greaseproof paper. Spread the mustard mixture over each half, then place one on top of the other, with the mustard mixture in the middle. Fold up the paper and twist the edges together tightly to seal.

4. Place in a steaming basket or large colander and steam for 20–25 minutes.

• CHICKEN WITH CHEESE AND HERB PURÉE •

SERVE these parcels unopened so that each person gets the full strength of the rich, fragrant aroma that wafts from the purée when the chicken is exposed. This is a perfect trouble-free recipe – after brief initial preparation, the chicken is put in the oven and can be forgotten while you prepare a vegetable accompaniment and a first course that requires more attention, such as Asparagus with Quick Hollandaise Sauce (see page 28) or Deep-fried Camembert (see page 27). For dessert you could serve Baked Apricots in Parcels with Vanilla (see page 102) or Baked Cinnamon Oranges (see page 103).

SERVES 4

4 skinless chicken breast fillets, each weighing about 150g (5oz)	55g (2oz) coarsely chopped mixed herbs such as basil, parsley, thyme and marjoram
salt and freshly ground black pepper	25g (1oz) soft cheese
2 shallots, chopped	15g (½oz) mature Cantal or Cheddar cheese, grated
1 clove garlic	about 75ml (3fl oz) virgin olive oil
1 tablespoon blanched almonds	

1. Preheat the oven to 200°C/400°F/Gas Mark 6 and put a baking sheet to heat.

2. Tear four pieces of foil each large enough to hold a piece of chicken. Season each breast and place on a piece of foil. Sprinkle with the chopped shallots.

3. Put the remaining ingredients, except the oil, in a small blender. With the motor running, slowly pour in sufficient oil to make a thick creamy purée with the consistency of mayonnaise.

4. Place equal amounts of the purée on each fillet, then loosely fold the foil over the chicken and seal the edges securely.

5. Put the foil parcels on the baking sheet and bake for 20–25 minutes.

· CHICKEN WITH FENNEL ·

THE aniseed flavour of fennel is a perfect foil to the mild taste of chicken, and when combined with lemon makes a lively dish.

SERVES 2

15g (½oz) unsalted butter
1 tablespoon olive oil
4 chicken drumsticks or thighs, or
   2 boneless chicken breasts
1 clove garlic
1 bulb fennel
salt and freshly ground black

pepper
3 tablespoons medium-bodied dry
   white wine, or water
juice of 1 lemon
2 tablespoons crème fraîche or
   soured cream

1. Heat the butter and oil in a frying pan, add the chicken and quickly brown all over.

2. Meanwhile, crush the garlic and thinly slice the fennel, reserving the feathery fronds. Stir the garlic, sliced fennel and seasoning into the pan for 2–3 minutes, then add the wine or water. Boil for a few seconds, lower the heat slightly and cook for 9–10 minutes until the chicken is tender and the fennel softened and lightly browned.

3. Using a slotted spoon, transfer the chicken to warmed plates, cover and keep warm. Stir the lemon juice and most of the fennel fronds into the pan, dislodging the sediment, then boil hard for about 2 minutes.

4. Remove the pan from the heat and stir in the crème fraîche or soured cream. Pour over the chicken, garnish with the remaining fennel fronds, and serve.

· GRILLED POUSSINS WITH ORANGE AND HERBS ·

ALTHOUGH it is not absolutely necessary to marinate the poussins before cooking, the flavour of the dish will be even better if they can be left for at least 15–30 minutes, or just while the grill is heating.

SERVES 2

100ml (3½fl oz) medium-bodied dry white wine
2 tablespoons olive oil
1 clove garlic, finely crushed
juice of 2 small oranges

1 teaspoon each chopped marjoram, thyme and rosemary
salt and freshly ground black pepper
2 poussins, each weighing about 550g (1¼lb)

1. Whisk together the wine, oil, garlic, orange juice, herbs and seasoning.

2. Preheat the grill if you are going to cook the birds right away.

3. Place the poussins on a board, breast-side down. Then, using sharp scissors, or game shears if you have them, cut through the backbone of each bird. Press on the breastbone with the heel of your hand, to break the bone and slightly flatten the poussin.

4. If there is time, marinate the poussins in the wine mixture for up to 2 hours.

5. Grill the poussins, skin-side up, basting frequently with the wine mixture, for 10–15 minutes. Turn the poussins, and grill for a further 10–15 minutes, basting occasionally. Serve with the juices poured over.

· Poussins with Shallot and Vinaigrette ·

For quicker cooking I use poussins that have been 'spatchcocked' – split along the backbone and flattened out. It takes very little time and is easy to do. But, if asked, a butcher will do it for you and it is sometimes possible to buy the birds ready-prepared from supermarkets.

SERVES 2

---

2 poussins, each weighing about
   450g (1lb)
unsalted butter
freshly ground black pepper
1 shallot

Vinaigrette
1 teaspoon Dijon or Bordeaux
   mustard
1–1½ tablespoons tarragon or white
   wine vinegar
4 tablespoons olive oil
salt and freshly ground black
   pepper

---

1. Preheat the grill.

2. Place the poussins on a board, breast-side down. Then, using sharp scissors, or game shears if you have them, cut through the backbone of each one. Flatten them slightly by pressing on the breastbone with the heel of your hand to break the bone. Rub a little butter over the skin and season with black pepper.

3. Grill the poussins, skin-side up, for 10–15 minutes. Turn the birds, baste with any cooking juices in the grill pan, and grill for a further 10–15 minutes, basting occasionally.

4. Meanwhile, finely chop the shallot. Whisk the mustard with the vinegar, then slowly pour in the oil, whisking constantly. Season.

5. Place the poussins skin-side down in a dish, and scatter over the chopped shallot. Then give the vinaigrette a quick whisk and immediately pour over the poussins. Cover tightly and leave to rest for 10 minutes while you have your first course.

· PIGEONS WITH THYME AND GARLIC ·

YOUNG, farmed pigeons, sometimes called 'squab', are tender and need far less cooking than the wild birds that generations of Frenchmen have enjoyed taking pot shots at.

SERVES 2

2 tablespoons olive oil
15g (½oz) butter
2 young farmed pigeons
10 cloves garlic, unpeeled
2 good sprigs of thyme

1 shallot
115ml (4fl oz) medium-bodied dry
  white wine
salt and freshly ground black
  pepper

1. Heat the oil and butter in a heavy flameproof casserole. Add the pigeons and brown them quickly and evenly, adding the garlic halfway through. Add the thyme, cover and cook for 10 minutes.

2. Meanwhile, finely chop the shallot.

3. Turn the pigeons over, add the chopped shallot, cover and cook for a further 10 minutes.

4. Transfer the pigeons, skin-side up, to a warmed serving plate, cover and keep warm.

5. Pour the fat from the casserole, leaving the garlic, thyme and shallot behind. Stir in the wine, dislodging the sediment, then boil until reduced by half. Add 4 tablespoons water and boil until the sauce has reduced to about 6 tablespoons. Season, pour over the pigeons, discard the thyme, and serve.

· DUCK WITH BLACK OLIVES ·

Duck breast fillets (French *magrets*) are quick to cook, as they are tender and usually served 'pink'. Most duck on sale now is leaner than it used to be, but you can always trim off the excess if there is more fat than you would like. To reduce the fat content further, you can wipe out the pan with paper towels after browning the duck.

For a special occasion or treat, use Barbary duck breasts as they have a particularly good flavour, as well as being plumper and less fatty than traditional Aylesbury ducks.

SERVES 2

2 duck breast fillets
1 orange
2 good sprigs of thyme
12 black olives in oil
200ml (7fl oz) chicken stock

1 tablespoon chopped parsley
15g (½oz) unsalted butter, diced
salt and freshly ground black
  pepper

---

1. With the point of a sharp knife, score the duck skin in a diamond pattern, taking care not to pierce the flesh. Heat a frying pan. Add the duck, skin-side down, and cook over a high heat until the skin is brown and crisp. Turn the duck over and brown the other side over a slightly lower heat for a further 3–4 minutes or until cooked to your liking.

2. Meanwhile, peel and thinly slice the orange. Add the orange slices to the pan with the thyme, olives and stock. Cover and cook gently until the duck is cooked to your liking.

3. Transfer the duck to a warmed plate, cover and keep warm. Add the parsley to the pan and boil hard until the liquid is reduced to 100ml (4fl oz). Whisk in the butter, season and pour over the duck.

· DUCK WITH PEACHES ·

THIS is a useful recipe (especially in summer when peaches are at their best) for when you want to cook something special quickly, either for guests or yourself.

SERVES 4

4 duck breast fillets
300ml (½ pint) medium-bodied dry
    white wine
about 55g (2oz) white sugar

2 ripe but firm peaches
4 tablespoons white wine vinegar
salt and freshly ground black
    pepper

1. Heat a heavy-based frying pan until very hot, while you use the point of a sharp knife to score through the skin and fat of each duck breast several times in a diamond pattern. Put the breasts, skin-side down, in the pan and cook over a high heat until the skin is brown and crisp. Turn the breasts over, lower the heat slightly and cook for a further 3–4 minutes or until cooked to your liking.

2. Meanwhile, in a separate pan, heat the wine and sugar to just on boiling point while you peel, halve and stone the peaches. Add the peaches to the wine and poach until just tender. Lift the peaches from the wine and keep warm; reserve the wine.

3. Transfer the duck to a warmed plate, cover and keep warm. Pour off the fat from the pan, then stir in the vinegar and boil until evaporated off. Stir in the reserved wine and reduce by half.

4. Slice the peaches and arrange with the duck on four warmed plates. Season the sauce, pour over the duck and peaches, and serve.

CHAPTER FOUR

VEGETABLES

VEGETABLE dishes should complement or enhance the main course, and for the cook in a hurry they can be a way of adding character to an otherwise simple meal of, for example, grilled lamb chops. With something firm and without a sauce, like the chops, choose a sauced or moist vegetable dish such as Quick Casseroled Flageolet Beans (see page 91).

Most fresh vegetables should, as far as possible, be bought every day, with the exception of staples such as potatoes and onions, and firmer vegetables like carrots, which can be kept in a cool place for a couple of days. As well as tasting so much better, fresh, small, tender vegetables cook more quickly than large, older ones.

Nowadays you do not have to spend time washing the mud from potatoes, leeks, spinach and lettuces, although you do have to spend more money. You can spend even more buying ready-sliced vegetables, but this really is a waste of money; their freshness, quality, texture and flavour start to deteriorate as soon as they are cut. Is it really worth saving the few minutes it would take to do the slicing, chopping or separating into florets yourself?

· CREAMED POTATOES WITH BASIL ·

FRENCH creamed potatoes are softer than the British equivalent. You need to mash the potatoes thoroughly with a masher – do not use a food processor or blender as the resulting purée will have a gluey consistency. Even better, if you have either, use a vegetable mill (*mouli légumes*) or a ricer. If you prefer, add 6 tablespoons olive oil instead of the butter.

SERVES 4

675g (1½lb) maincrop potatoes, such as King Edward, Maris Piper or Golden Wonder
salt and freshly ground black pepper

leaves from a large bunch of basil
75g (3oz) unsalted butter
100ml (3½fl oz) milk
4–6 tablespoons crème fraîche or double cream

1. Heat a large frying pan containing just enough water to cover the potatoes. Meanwhile, peel and chop the potatoes, add to the water and bring quickly to the boil. Add salt, cover and simmer for about 15 minutes until the potatoes are tender.

2. Put the basil leaves into a bowl and cut them with scissors. Dice the butter.

3. Tip the potatoes into a colander to drain. Put the pan over a low heat, add the butter and basil and heat until the basil is soft.

4. Add most of the milk to the pan and mash the potatoes thoroughly in a bowl. Lightly beat the potatoes into the milk, then whisk them. Whisk in the remaining milk and crème fraîche or cream. Season and serve.

VARIATION

Creamed Potatoes with Goat's Cheese
Follow the main recipe but use 175g (6oz) soft goat's cheese instead of the basil (or you could use them both). Warm the cheese gently with the crème fraîche or cream, then whisk into the potato. Season with plenty of black pepper.

· QUICK POTATO GRATIN ·

POTATO gratins are usually served as a vegetable accompaniment, but I also like this version, which contains leeks as well, for a light vegetarian lunch or supper dish, accompanied by a crisp green salad and good firm bread.

SERVES 4

450g (1lb) even-sized potatoes, peeled if liked
2 leeks, sliced
about 40g (1½oz) mature Cantal or Cheddar cheese

150ml (5fl oz) crème fraîche, whipping cream or thick plain yogurt
salt and freshly ground black pepper

1. Bring some water to boil in a saucepan – you only need enough water to cover the potatoes by about 2.5cm (1 inch).

2. Cut the potatoes into 5mm (¼ inch) slices, add to the pan, cover and return quickly to the boil. Simmer for about 7 minutes until just tender.

3. Slice the leeks and add to the pan for the last 1–2 minutes.

4. Meanwhile, preheat the grill and warm a shallow heatproof dish. Finely grate the cheese, and gently warm the crème fraîche, cream or yogurt in a small saucepan.

5. Tip the vegetables into a colander to drain, then transfer to the dish and arrange in an even layer. Season the crème fraîche, cream or yogurt and pour over the vegetables. Sprinkle over the cheese and put under the grill until bubbling and golden brown.

· JACKET ONIONS ·

SERVE two onions per person as a vegetable accompaniment, or three for a lunch or supper dish embellished with a dollop of goat's cheese.

SERVES 2–4

8–9 onions, each weighing about
   75g (3oz), unpeeled
3 tablespoons olive oil
salt and freshly ground black
   pepper

a small nut of butter (optional)
chopped parsley or tarragon
   (optional)

1. Preheat the oven to 220°C/425°F/Gas Mark 7. Place the onions in a small roasting tin or shallow baking dish. Spoon over the oil, and season.

2. Bake on the top shelf of the oven for about 30 minutes or until soft.

3. Serve the onions split open with extra black pepper ground over the cut surfaces. If liked, top with a nut of butter and a sprinkling of chopped parsley or tarragon.

· GLAZED SHALLOTS ·

TO SPEED the peeling of the shallots, pour boiling water over them, leave for about 5 minutes, then drain and peel.

SERVES 4

300g (10oz) shallots, peeled
40g (1½oz) unsalted butter

salt and freshly ground black
   pepper

1. Put the shallots in a saucepan, cover with cold water and bring to the boil. Boil for 5 minutes, then drain.

2. Heat the butter in a frying pan, add the shallots and seasoning, cover and cook, shaking the pan frequently, for 10 minutes or until they are tender and well-glazed.

· CARROTS VICHY ·

THE water from the springs of Vichy in central France, has a high bicarbonate of soda content which, when combined with the butter and parsley, gives a characteristic flavour to this simple light way of cooking carrots. The carrots, which should be young, tender and fresh, are usually sliced diagonally.

SERVES 4

450g (1lb) small carrots, sliced
    diagonally
a small pinch of bicarbonate of
    soda

25g (1oz) unsalted butter, diced
2 teaspoons caster sugar
salt
1 tablespoon chopped parsley

1. Put the carrots in a heavy-based saucepan, just cover with water, and add the bicarbonate of soda. Bring to the boil, then simmer, shaking the pan occasionally, for 10–12 minutes, until the carrots are tender and nearly all the liquid has evaporated.

2. Add the butter, sugar and a small pinch of salt and continue to cook, tossing the pan frequently, until the carrots are lightly glazed. Serve sprinkled with the parsley.

· COURGETTES WITH HERBS ·

FOR real speed, steam the courgettes until tender, then simply toss with diced butter, thyme, lemon juice and seasoning.

SERVES 4

450g (1lb) small courgettes
about 25–40g (1–1½oz) unsalted
  butter, diced
2 tablespoons chopped thyme, or
  mixed basil and parsley

salt and freshly ground black
  pepper
juice of ½ lemon

1. Bring a steamer, or a saucepan, a third filled with water, to the boil.

2. Meanwhile, thinly slice the courgettes and spread out in a steaming basket. Place the basket over the steamer base or saucepan, cover, and steam for 1–2 minutes until almost tender.

3. Melt the butter in a separate pan, add the courgettes, stir to coat with butter, sprinkle with the herbs and seasoning, cover and continue to cook over a low heat, shaking the pan occasionally, until the courgettes are tender. Squeeze over the lemon juice and serve.

VARIATION

Courgettes with Almonds

1. Fry 450g (1lb) thinly sliced small courgettes and 4–6 tablespoons flaked almonds in 50g (2oz) unsalted butter and 2 tablespoons olive oil. Stir frequently, until the courgettes are golden and beginning to soften but still crunchy.

2. Season, squeeze over some lemon juice and serve with the pan juices.

· COURGETTES WITH TOMATOES ·

IT IS always worth selecting small courgettes because large ones do not taste as good and they exude more water, quickly becoming soft and limp rather than crisp and tender. Start by frying some chopped shallot, spring onion or onion if you like.

―――――――――――――――― SERVES 4 ――――――――――――――――

20g (¾oz) unsalted butter, diced
1 tablespoon olive oil
300g (10oz) small courgettes, thinly sliced
300g (10oz) well-flavoured tomatoes

1–2 tablespoons chopped tarragon
salt and freshly ground black pepper

1. Heat the butter and oil in a frying pan, add the courgettes and cook for 3–4 minutes until just softened, stirring occasionally.

2. Meanwhile, peel the tomatoes if liked (see page 44), and seed and chop them.

3. Add the tomatoes to the pan with the tarragon and seasoning. Shake the pan until the tomatoes are warm, then serve.

· CREAMED LEEKS ·

FROMAGE frais or a low- or medium-fat soft cheese can be used in place of crème fraîche or soured cream.

―――――――――――――――― SERVES 4 ――――――――――――――――

550g (1¼lb) slim leeks
25g (1oz) unsalted butter, diced
3 tablespoons crème fraîche or soured cream

salt and freshly ground black pepper
1–2 tablespoons chopped parsley

1. Slit the leeks lengthways, then chop or slice them.

2. Heat the butter in a frying pan, add the leeks and fry, stirring frequently, until the leeks have softened slightly but retain some texture.

3. Stir in the crème fraîche or soured cream, and seasoning, using plenty of black pepper. Bubble briefly to thicken slightly, and serve with chopped parsley.

· QUICK CASSEROLED FLAGEOLET BEANS ·

TRADITIONALLY this dish is cooked slowly in a thick, covered pot, but I have made a quick version using canned flageolet beans. For a richer dish that is better as a main course rather than as an accompaniment, replace the tomatoes with 5 tablespoons crème fraîche and 65g (2½oz) fromage frais or soft cheese. Canned, or cooked, green or brown lentils can be substituted for the flageolet beans.

SERVES 2

25g (1oz) unsalted butter, diced
1 onion, finely chopped
1–2 cloves garlic, chopped
1 × 400g (14oz) can flageolet beans
leaves from 3 sprigs of thyme
1 bay leaf, torn in half

leaves from 4 sprigs of tarragon
2 large well-flavoured tomatoes, peeled if liked (see page 44), seeded and coarsely chopped
salt and freshly ground black pepper
chopped parsley

1. Heat the butter in a saucepan, add the onion and garlic and cook fairly slowly until soft and golden brown.

2. Meanwhile, drain and rinse the beans. Place in a medium saucepan and just cover with water. Heat through.

3. Drain the beans and add to the onion and garlic, together with the herbs, tomatoes, salt and plenty of black pepper. Heat, stirring occasionally, so the tomatoes are warm. Serve sprinkled with parsley.

· CHERRY TOMATOES WITH HERBS ·

THE tomatoes should only be warmed through, which doesn't take long. They are best served immediately, so don't add them to the pan until shortly before they are needed.

Use some, not all of the herbs I've mentioned, using less of the stronger-flavoured mint, basil and tarragon. Serve with grilled chicken or lamb.

SERVES 4

25g (1oz) unsalted butter, diced, or 2 tablespoons olive oil
2 shallots, finely chopped
550g (1¼lb) ripe but firm well-flavoured cherry tomatoes, halved or quartered depending on size

about 1 tablespoon chopped mixed herbs such as thyme, parsley, chervil, mint, basil and tarragon
salt and freshly ground black pepper

1. Heat the butter or oil in a wide frying pan, add the chopped shallots and cook for 1–1½ minutes.

2. Add the tomatoes, increase the heat and cook quickly until warmed, shaking the pan frequently. Take care not to overcook, otherwise the tomatoes will begin to stew and the skins toughen.

3. Add the herbs and seasoning, and serve immediately.

· BRAISED SAVOURY CABBAGE ·

DON'T be deterred by the length of the method – it's long because the preparation of all the ingredients is done in a succession of operations that conveniently and neatly slot together.

Serve as a light lunch or supper dish (omit the bacon or ham and add extra cheese for vegetarians), or as an accompaniment to simple grilled beef or lamb. If serving as a side dish, the cabbage can be left to cook while you prepare the main course.

SERVES 4

2 tablespoons olive oil
100g (3½oz) lardons or thick piece
   of streaky bacon or ham
1 onion
1–2 cloves garlic (optional)
550g (1¼lb) savoy cabbage
a sprig of thyme

3 sun-dried tomato halves or 2 large
   well-flavoured tomatoes
115g (4oz) Gruyère cheese
25g (1oz) Parmesan cheese or soft
   goat's cheese
salt and freshly ground black
   pepper

1. Heat the oil in a large frying pan while cutting the bacon or ham into cubes. Add the bacon or ham or lardons to the pan and leave to cook while you chop the onion. Stir this into the pan and fry until softened.

2. Crush the garlic, if used, add to the pan, then shred the cabbage. Stir the cabbage and thyme into the pan until starting to wilt.

3. If using sun-dried tomatoes, cut them into strips; seed and chop fresh tomatoes. Add the tomatoes to the cabbage, cover and leave to cook, shaking the pan occasionally, for about 10–15 minutes.

4. Dice the Gruyère, and soft goat's cheese, if using, and grate the Parmesan. Stir the cheeses into the pan with plenty of black pepper – salt may not be necessary because of the salt in the bacon or ham, sun-dried tomatoes and cheese.

5. Serve very hot, in a warm serving dish, when the Gruyère starts melting into strings.

· BUTTERED CABBAGE ·

IN BRITAIN we tend to think of cabbage as invariably boiled and over-cooked. However, whereas we view cabbage as a humble vegetable worthy only of derision, across the Channel they respect it and exercise sympathy when cooking it. In this way they produce a great variety of, believe it or not, delicious cabbage dishes, such as this very simple one.

SERVES 4

1 small firm cabbage	1 nutmeg
65–75g (2½–3oz) unsalted butter	freshly ground black pepper

1. Bring 2cm (¾ inch) salted water to the boil in a large saucepan.

2. Meanwhile, thinly shred the cabbage. Add the cabbage to the saucepan, cover and boil vigorously until almost cooked.

3. Tip the cabbage into a colander to drain well. Return the pan to the heat. Dice the butter, add to the pan and swirl it. Add the cabbage, grate in a little nutmeg and add plenty of black pepper. Cover and cook for a few minutes, shaking the pan occasionally, until the cabbage is just tender.

4. Stir everything around so the cabbage is well coated in butter, and serve immediately; this is important.

· CAULIFLOWER AND BLUE CHEESE PARCELS ·

CAULIFLOWER and cheese sauce is a well-known and well-loved partnership, but there is no need to go to the trouble of making a cheese sauce to enjoy the combination. If you top cauliflower with diced Roquefort, goat's cheese and butter, enclose in a parcel and pop in the oven, the cheese and butter will melt and fuse together to bathe the cauliflower in a buttery, piquant, self-made sauce. The parcels can be prepared in advance and baked when required. Serve them unopened.

Although I usually make this dish as a vegetable accompaniment, I also sometimes prepare it for a first course, or a light lunch or supper dish to eat with good, crusty bread.

SERVES 4

2 shallots	olive oil
450g (1lb) cauliflower florets	75g (3oz) Roquefort cheese
2 sprigs of parsley	75g (3oz) soft goat's cheese
1 bay leaf	25–40g (1–1½oz) unsalted butter
2 sprigs of thyme	freshly ground black pepper

1. Preheat the oven to 190°C/375°F/Gas Mark 5. Put enough water in a saucepan to just cover the cauliflower, and bring to the boil.

2. Meanwhile, finely chop the shallots and add these to the boiling water with the cauliflower. Put the lid on the pan and return quickly to the boil. Coarsely chop the parsley, tear the bay leaf across and strip the leaves from the thyme, then add all the herbs to the pan. Simmer until the cauliflower is just starting to become tender.

3. Tear or cut four pieces of foil and brush with olive oil. Tip the cauliflower into a colander and discard the bay leaf. Divide the cauliflower between the pieces of foil, then dot with the cheeses and butter. Add plenty of black pepper, fold up the sides of the foil and seal the edges tightly.

4. Place the parcels on a baking sheet, bake for about 15 minutes, and serve unopened.

· CRUMBED BROCCOLI ·

THERE are two main types of broccoli – sprouting broccoli, which I think has the finer flavour, and broccoli calabrese, the thick-stemmed type that accounts for most fresh broccoli on sale, especially in supermarkets. Don't waste the thick stems – peel off skin if it seems tough, then cut the stems into slices about 1.25cm (½ inch) thick and put them to cook for 2–3 minutes before adding the florets.

––––––– SERVES 4 –––––––

450g (1lb) broccoli florets
2 tablespoons olive oil
25g (1oz) unsalted butter, diced
2 cloves garlic
25g (1oz) fine fresh breadcrumbs
2 tablespoons finely chopped
    parsley

2 tablespoons freshly grated mature
    Cantal or Parmesan cheese
    (optional)
salt and freshly ground black
    pepper

1. Steam the broccoli in a covered steaming basket or colander over boiling salted water for about 3–4 minutes or until tender but still crisp.

2. Meanwhile, heat the oil and butter in a frying pan. Finely chop the garlic and add to the pan with the breadcrumbs. Fry over a moderate heat, stirring frequently, until the crumbs are golden.

3. Tip the broccoli into a warmed serving dish. Stir the parsley into the crumbs, pour over the broccoli, sprinkle with the cheese, if using, and season with salt and plenty of black pepper.

VARIATION

Alternatively, cook the broccoli as above and serve with Quick Hollandaise Sauce (see page 28).

Opposite: Sausages Braised with Lentils (page 70) and Pumpkin au Gratin (page 99)

· CREAMED BROAD BEANS ·

THIS is a very useful recipe as it provides plenty of scope for adaptation. For example, it can be made into a stronger-tasting dish by frying chopped shallot, spring onion or onion in the butter, and perhaps mixing in some diced ham; the addition of diced red pepper will add a splash of colour as well as flavour.

SERVES 4

450g (1lb) frozen or fresh baby
  broad beans
salt and freshly ground black
  pepper
20g (¾oz) unsalted butter

¾–1 teaspoon chopped savory or
  leaves from a few sprigs of
  tarragon, chopped
2 tablespoons crème fraîche or
  soured cream

1. Put just enough water to cover the beans in a wide frying pan or saucepan and bring to the boil. Add the beans, cover the pan and return quickly to the boil. Add salt, then simmer for 5–7 minutes until just tender.

2. Drain the beans. Swirl the butter into the pan, then gently stir in the beans to coat them with butter without breaking them up. Add the savory or tarragon, crème fraîche or soured cream, and seasoning. Shake the pan to distribute the crème fraîche or sour cream, and serve.

Opposite: Summer Fruit Gratin (page 101) and Baked Apricots en Papillote with Vanilla (page 102)

· BRAISED PEAS WITH LETTUCE ·

Braising peas with lettuce used to be a way of coaxing garden peas that had passed the first flush of youth, back to sweet tenderness. Such ploys are not necessary for frozen peas, but this is, nevertheless, a good way of cooking them. (If you try the recipe with garden peas, cook them for longer, depending on their age.)

As the recipe stands, it makes a light, fresh vegetable accompaniment but for extra character you could add cooked ham with the spring onions, and/or sprinkle the peas with finely chopped parsley, or use mint if you haven't added ham.

—————————————— SERVES 4 ——————————————

about 5 leaves from a round lettuce
40–55g (1½–2oz) unsalted butter
4 spring onions, chopped
350g (12oz) frozen peas
3 tablespoons vegetable or chicken
   stock, medium-bodied dry white
   wine, or water

a few sprigs of parsley
salt and freshly ground black
   pepper

1. Lay the lettuce leaves on top of each other, roll them up, then cut across into slices.

2. Swirl half the butter in a frying pan or wide saucepan until melted, then add the spring onions and lettuce. Stir for about 2 minutes until the lettuce has wilted, then add the peas, the stock, wine or water, and the parsley. Cover tightly and cook gently, shaking the pan occasionally, until the peas are tender.

3. Add the remaining butter, and the seasoning. Serve the peas with the cooking juices poured over.

· PUMPKIN AU GRATIN ·

PUMPKINS and squash are now becoming fashionable here, but they have been a staple in much of rural France for generations – I have a booklet from one region that gives 150 different pumpkin recipes. Pumpkins are quite commonly grown in allotments and vegetable gardens, but one of the most unusual sights I've seen was a face carved on a still-growing pumpkin!

Serve with crusty bread as a starter or vegetarian main dish, or as an accompaniment to grilled meat or poultry.

SERVES 2

1 butternut squash
2¼ teaspoons thyme
1 clove garlic
40g (1½oz) mixed Gruyère and
    Parmesan cheese
melted unsalted butter

75ml (3fl oz) crème fraîche
salt and freshly ground black
    pepper
1 tablespoon chopped parsley
extra grated Parmesan cheese

1. Cook the squash in a large saucepan of boiling water for about 7–10 minutes, or until a wooden toothpick slides in easily.

2. Meanwhile, preheat the grill. Chop the thyme and garlic. Grate the Gruyère cheese, finely grate the Parmesan, and mix the two together.

3. Drain the squash. Then, protecting your hands with a cloth, cut it in half lengthways, scoop out the seeds and cut several slashes in the concave part of the flesh where the seeds were.

4. Place the squash halves, cut-side up, in a shallow baking dish. Brush the cut surfaces with melted butter and sprinkle with the thyme and garlic. Pour the crème fraîche into the hollow left by the seeds, sprinkle over the cheese, season, and place under the grill until the cheese has melted and is tinged with gold.

5. Serve sprinkled with parsley and accompanied by extra grated Parmesan cheese.

CHAPTER FIVE

DESSERTS

MANY PEOPLE like to end a meal with something sweet, but making a full-scale pudding is not always practical or desirable. I find that fruit, a popular ending to family meals in France, provides the basis of most quick desserts I make. These satisfy both those who want some form of pudding and those who prefer something light and fresh. They are also very simple to assemble and need only minimal cooking, if any. In most cases they can be finished off after the main course has been eaten.

· SUMMER FRUIT GRATIN ·

A DISH of cool, juicy, fragrant fruit beneath a chilled blanket of voluptuous crème fraîche, gilded with hot, crisp, bitter-sweet caramelised sugar, sends many people into raptures. My favourite fruit gratins are made with summer fruits, such as strawberries, raspberries, black and red currants and peaches. Other fruits that provide a fruity-sharp, succulent contrast to the crème fraîche, such as oranges, soft citrus, plums, and cooked blackberry and apple, also work well.

Don't be too mean with the sugar, otherwise there will not be enough to make a sufficiently thick layer of caramel to provide the necessary contrast to the crème fraîche. (Don't forget that sugar loses some of its sweetness when caramelised.) A good layer of sugar also protects the crème fraîche from the heat, keeping it cool and preventing it bubbling up, again maintaining that vital contrast. If you prefer, you can use thick yogurt instead of part or all of the crème fraîche, or use a mixture of thick yogurt and fromage frais.

SERVES 4

about 550g (1¼lb) chilled prepared mixed summer fruits, such as strawberries, raspberries, black and red currants and peaches

about 225ml (8fl oz) crème fraîche, chilled
about 150g (5oz) caster sugar

1. Preheat the grill to very hot, and arrange the fruit in a heatproof dish. Spread the crème fraîche over the fruit, then completely cover with a layer of sugar at least 3mm (⅛inch) thick – make sure there are no gaps around the edge.

2. Place the dish close to the grill so that the sugar very quickly melts and caramelises. Serve immediately.

· BAKED APRICOTS EN PAPILLOTE WITH VANILLA ·

ORANGE and vanilla highlight the flavour of apricots, so baking them with orange and a little vanilla pod, is an excellent way of livening up apricots that are not as well-flavoured and juicy as one would hope. I learnt this recipe while staying on a farm in the Chablis region of France.

For extra oomph, add some Cognac, rum, Cointreau (an orange liqueur made on the banks of the Loire), or an almond liqueur. If, after baking, you feel some sweetness is necessary, add a little clear honey.

SERVES 4

12 ripe apricots
1 vanilla pod, broken into 4 pieces

1 orange
clear honey (optional)

1. Preheat the oven to 200°C/400°F/Gas Mark 6. Butter four large pieces of greaseproof paper or foil. Cut the apricots in half, following the natural indentations, then twist out the stones. Pile six apricot halves on each piece of greaseproof paper.

2. Place a piece of vanilla pod on each pile of apricots. Grate the orange rind over the apricots, then cut the orange in half and squeeze the juice over them. Fold the greaseproof paper or foil over each pile and twist the edges together to seal tightly.

3. Place on a baking sheet and bake for about 10 minutes. Serve hot, placing each parcel on an individual serving plate. Serve honey separately, if wished.

VARIATION

Baked Cinnamon Oranges
1. Preheat the oven to 200°C/400°F/Gas Mark 6. Using a sharp knife, pare the peel and pith from 4 oranges. Slice each orange, then divide the slices between four pieces of greaseproof paper or foil.

2. Break a cinnamon stick into four pieces and place a piece on each pile of orange slices. Trickle over each about 1½ teaspoons good-quality clear honey and 1 teaspoon Cointreau or Cognac.

3. Fold up the greaseproof paper or foil, twisting the edges together tightly to seal. Then place the parcels on a baking sheet and bake for 7–10 minutes until the oranges are heated through.

4. Serve the oranges in their parcels, on their own or with cool crème fraîche to complement the warm, spicy-sweet-sharp oranges.

· STRAWBERRY CREAM ·

I KNOW we can now have strawberries all year round, but I'm a traditionalist and still think they are essentially a summer fruit. It is only then that they can ripen naturally, basking for long days beneath a warm sun. I had some plump, fruity, juicy ones served in this way when I had an impromptu meal with some friends who live on the outskirts of Carcassonne. We ate in the kitchen and the dessert was brought together as we watched, after we had eaten the main course. It was heavenly.

SERVES 4

350g (12oz) ripe strawberries
115ml (4fl oz) crème fraîche, chilled
225g (½lb) fromage frais, chilled

icing sugar (optional)
crisp almond biscuits

---

1. Crush the strawberries with a fork.

2. Stir the crème fraîche into the fromage frais, then gently fold into the strawberries. Sweeten with icing sugar, if liked.

3. Spoon into cold glasses and serve with almond biscuits.

· STUFFED FIGS WITH RASPBERRY SAUCE ·

I HAVE always eaten a lot of all types of fruit (except bananas) so when I was working on the outskirts of Burgundy recently I was in my element. From late July onwards the nearby Joigny market sold fruit such as figs and white and yellow peaches and nectarines which seemed like totally different species to their counterparts sold in Britain.

I like to eat fresh fruit on its own, but when I'm cooking for others this is one of the best ways I know of making a smart but easy dessert.

SERVES 4

225g (½lb) raspberries
lemon juice
icing sugar
115g (4oz) fromage frais, chilled

about 4 tablespoons crème fraîche, chilled
rose water (optional)
8 large ripe figs

1. Press the raspberries through a non-metallic sieve, then add lemon juice and icing sugar to taste. Place in the refrigerator.

2. Beat the fromage frais. Lightly beat the crème fraîche, then fold into the fromage frais and flavour with a few drops of rose water, if liked.

3. Cut the figs almost into quarters from stem to base, leaving the sections joined at the base. Ease the sections apart. Stand two figs on each of four small plates, and spoon fromage frais mixture into each fig.

4. Trickle a little of the raspberry sauce over the filling, pour the remainder around the figs and serve.

VARIATION

Peaches with Raspberry Sauce

1. Prepare the raspberry sauce as above, adding a few drops of Raspberry Eau de Vie or Kirsch, if liked.

2. Pour boiling water over 4 large ripe peaches. After 10 seconds, then drain and slip off the skins. Or the peaches can be left unpeeled.

3. Cut the peaches into halves and remove the stones. Pour the sauce over the peaches, and serve.

· FRUITS IN WINE ·

COOL and fruity, and frivolous if sparkling wine is used, Fruits in Wine, for me, is an ideal summer dessert, redolent of many happy days of relaxed eating of the best, invariably simple, foods that France has to offer. Although it takes mere minutes to assemble, if you really have been short of time, just place the fruit on the table and leave the guests to prepare it themselves, then dip it in their wine.

Strawberries in Sparkling or Sweet White Wine

Drink the rest of the bottle of wine with the dessert. Instead of sparkling wine, you could use a dessert wine such as Muscat de Beaumes de Venise or a sweet Vouvray.

SERVES 4

---

about 550g (1¼lb) ripe strawberries
icing or caster sugar
about ½ bottle chilled medium-
    bodied sparkling white wine, such
    as Vouvray

macaroons

---

1. Hull and halve, quarter or slice the strawberries into glasses or dessert bowls. Sieve or sprinkle over a little sugar to taste, and refrigerate while eating the rest of the meal.

2. Just before serving, pour over the wine. Serve accompanied by macaroons.

Peaches in White Wine

Pour boiling water over 4 ripe peaches, leave for about 20 seconds then remove the peaches from the water and peel off their skins. Halve the peaches, remove the stones, then reassemble the peaches (you could put some home-made marzipan, or a strawberry or raspberry in the cavity). Proceed as above.

Strawberries in Red Wine

After sweetening the strawberries, sprinkle a fruity, quite light red wine, such as Chinon, Bourgeuil or Beaujolais, over them.

· PEARS POACHED IN RED WINE ·

Sᴇʀᴠᴇᴅ warm, I think this is an especially welcome dessert for chilly autumn or winter days when you want something that is warming without being heavy. The lightly sweetened and spiced rich red wine beautifully complements the pale juiciness of the fruity pears.

——————————— SERVES 4 ———————————

about 3–4 tablespoons crème de
   cassis, or sugar
2 cloves
½ cinnamon stick
300ml (½ pint) fruity red wine

4 ripe but firm Williams or Comice
   pears
lemon juice (optional)
crème fraîche or Greek-style yogurt

1. Put the crème de cassis or sugar, the cloves, cinnamon and wine in a deep saucepan, just large enough to hold the pears, and gently heat.

2. Meanwhile, peel the pears, leaving the stalks on.

3. Stand the pears upright in the saucepan. Baste the pears a few times with the wine. Then cover and simmer gently for about 10 minutes, depending on the fruit's firmness, until the pears are just tender, basting occasionally with the wine.

4. Using a slotted spoon, transfer the pears to a serving bowl. Taste the wine and remove the spices if the flavour is sufficiently spicy.

5. Boil the wine hard until reduced by half, then adjust the sweetness if necessary by adding more crème de cassis or sugar. If it needs sharpening, add some lemon juice.

6. Remove the spices, if you haven't already done so, and pour the wine over the pears. Serve with crème fraîche or Greek-style yogurt.

· HOT BUTTERED APPLES IN ORANGE SAUCE ·

ALTHOUGH I have driven under banners proclaiming French fairs in honour of 'Granny' (Granny Smith apples), Reine de Reinette and Reinette apples are still France's favourite varieties for eating and cooking.

Butter is a much better medium than water for cooking apples if they are to be eaten hot. A small pinch of ground cinnamon mixed with the sugar goes well with Reinette apples (and our Coxs if you can't find Reinettes).

SERVES 2

2 good-sized, well-flavoured dessert apples, such as Reinette or Cox's Orange Pippin
55g (2oz) unsalted butter, diced

2 tablespoons light soft brown sugar
1 large orange
a dash of Calvados or brandy (optional)

---

1. Halve and core the apples, then cut each half into four wedges.

2. Melt the butter in a wide, shallow, preferably non-stick, pan. Put the apples in the pan in a single layer and cook until pale gold underneath. Turn the wedges over carefully, sprinkle with the sugar and continue to cook until the underside is golden and the apples have softened.

3. Meanwhile, finely grate the rind from the orange, and squeeze the juice.

4. Using a slotted spoon, transfer the apples to warmed serving plates, cover and keep warm.

5. Stir the Calvados or brandy, if using, into the pan and set it alight with a taper. When the flames die down, stir in the orange juice and rind, bubble until slightly thickened, then pour over the apples and serve hot.

· CARAMELISED PEARS ON TOASTED BRIOCHE ·

AS BRIOCHE is made with butter, there is no need to spread the cut slices with butter. That way, it stays crisp. If you do not have any brioche, milk or egg bread can be used instead, but you may find that you prefer it buttered rather than plain – try it both ways.

SERVES 4

4 ripe but firm pears
2 tablespoons Calvados or Cognac,
 or juice of ½ lemon
about 25–40g (1–1½oz) unsalted
 butter

4 slices brioche, about 1.25cm
 (½ inch) thick
2 tablespoons blanched almonds,
 halved
icing sugar

1. Peel the pears, cut them in half lengthways and remove the cores. Slice one half lengthways several times, almost to the neck, then press down lightly on the pear so the slices fan out. Repeat with the remaining halves.

2. Put the pears in a shallow dish or on a plate, sprinkle over the Calvados or Cognac, or squeeze over the lemon juice, and leave for as long as you can.

3. Preheat the grill to very hot. Gently melt the butter in a small saucepan.

4. Place the brioche slices in a shallow baking dish or tin, then place half a pear on each slice. Brush with melted butter, scatter the almonds over, then cover with a generous dusting of icing sugar. Grill for 5–7 minutes until the sugar has caramelised and the pears are golden.

VARIATION

Alternatively, use 4 apples (such as Reinette or Cox's Orange Pippin) instead of pears; you can peel the apples or not, as you prefer. Proceed as above, except that you need to slice the apples and arrange the slices, slightly overlapping, on the brioche.

· CHOCOLATE MOUSSE ·

A LUSCIOUS mousse that will please even the choosiest of chocolate aficionados can be made in just a few minutes. But you must use decent chocolate – that is, one with a cocoa butter content of at least 55 per cent (good supermarkets sell them).

You can flavour the mousse with strong black coffee, orange, mint or coffee liqueur, or finely grated orange rind. And you can enhance its appearance with a swirl of whipped cream, perhaps flavoured with crème de menthe or a couple of drops of peppermint essence and a little icing sugar if you haven't flavoured the mousse.

SERVES 2

115g (4oz) good-quality plain chocolate

2 eggs
a small knob of unsalted butter

1. Heat a small saucepan of water with a bowl placed over, but not in, the water. Break the chocolate into small pieces, place in the bowl and leave until beginning to soften.

2. Meanwhile, separate the eggs.

3. Stir the chocolate until smooth, then stir in the butter and remove the bowl from the heat. Stir in the egg yolks.

4. Whisk the egg whites until stiff but not dry. Then lightly and gently fold in the chocolate mixture, using a metal spoon.

5. Divide the mixture between two chilled individual dishes or glasses and place in the refrigerator while you eat the rest of the meal.

INDEX